Consciousness, Color, and Content

Representation and Mind
Hilary Putnam and Ned Block, editors

Consciousness, Color, and Content

Michael Tye

A Bradford Book
The MIT Press
Cambridge, Massachusetts
London, England

First MIT Press paperback edition, 2002
©2000 Massachusetts Institute of Technology

This book was set in Sabon by Best-set Typesetter Ltd., Hong Kong.

Printed and bound in the United States of America.

Library of Congress Cataloging-in-Publication Data

Tye, Michael.
  Consciousness, color, and content / Michael Tye.
     p. cm.
  "A Bradford book."
  Includes bibliographical references and index.
  ISBN 0-262-20129-1 (hc : alk. paper), 0-262-70088-3 (pb)
  1. Consciousness.   2. Color (Philosophy)   3. Mental representation.
I. Title.

  B808.9 .T94 2000
  126–dc21   99-089688

For Cecily

Contents

Preface

Experiences and feelings are inherently conscious states. This is not to say that if I am undergoing an experience or feeling, I must be attending to it; my attention is often focused elsewhere. Still, if I have an experience or feeling, consciousness must surely be present. Consciousness of this sort goes with talk of "raw feels," of "sensational qualities," of "what it is like." For a person who feels pain, there is something it is *like* for him to be in pain. *Phenomenal* consciousness is present.

Phenomenal consciousness is *essential* or *integral* to experiences and feelings in a way in which it is not to other mental states. The state of thinking that water is wet, to take a specific case, has no characteristic phenomenal "feel," in my view, although it may certainly be accompanied by a linguistic, auditory image with phenomenal features. The subject of the thought may "hear" an inner voice. It may seem to the subject as if she is uttering a sentence in her native language, complete with a certain pattern of stress and intonation. Remove the phenomenology of the auditory experience, however, and no phenomenology remains.[1]

I currently have a rich and varied phenomenal consciousness. My visual field is full of the colors of my garden. I have auditory sensations of a bird singing from a nearby tree. I feel my watch strap on my wrist and my shirt sleeves on my arms. I have a dryness in my mouth, a soreness in my right knee. I feel my feet touching the floor, my hands resting upon my legs, my brow furrow as I think about what to write. Sensory experiences such as these can (and do) exist whether or not their subjects are attending to them.[2]

Phenomenal consciousness seems to be a relatively primitive, largely automatic matter, something more widespread in nature than higher-order consciousness, for example. But it is also deeply puzzling. In Tye 1995, I elaborated and defended a theory of phenomenal consciousness that has come to be known as representationalism. In reflecting further upon the view, and in responding to questions at talks and in discussions, I have come to realize that there are aspects to representationalism that need further clarification (and indeed aspects that need certain minor revisions). For example, it seems to me that the so-called "transparency intuition," which undeniably plays a very important role in motivating the representationalist view, has not been well understood; nor has the notion of content, in terms of which phenomenal character or "feel" is best elucidated. I have also come to think that it would be worthwhile not only to offer detailed replies to certain recalcitrant objections to representationalism but also to connect the view with other issues of philosophical interest (most notably, the question of the nature of color).

My focus in the essays that comprise this book is broader than representationalism and associated topics, however. Two prominent challenges for *any* reductive theory of consciousness are the explanatory gap and the knowledge argument. Much has been written on these challenges (I myself have not been reticent [Tye 1984, 1995]), but more remains to be said. In particular, it now seems to me that the two challenges are intimately related and that the best strategy for dealing with the explanatory gap is to argue that it is a kind of cognitive illusion. Part I of the book is concerned with these more general matters.

Part II is devoted to representationalism itself. This part opens with a summary of representationalism and its motivations. I have tried to make the development of the view here especially clear, and I think that this chapter contains enough new material (as well as some minor revisions) to make it worthwhile to peruse even for those who are fully familiar with the theory presented in Tye 1995. The three chapters that follow deal with objections to representationalism that take the form of putative counterexamples.

The first class of these consists of actual, real-world cases in which, it is claimed, perceptual experiences are the same representationally but different phenomenally. These are the focus of chapter 4. Another class of objections consists of imaginary cases in which experiences supposedly are identical representationally but inverted phenomenally. These cases, along with a modified representational theory proposed by Sydney Shoemaker, are the focus of chapter 5. A third class of putative counterexamples consists of problem cases in which experiences allegedly have different representational contents (of the relevant sort) but the same phenomenal character. Ned Block's Inverted Earth example (1990) is of this type. Counterexamples are also sometimes given in which supposedly experience of one sort or another is present but in which there is no state with representational content. Swampman—the molecule-by-molecule replica of a notable philosopher (Donald Davidson), formed accidentally by the chemical reaction that occurs in a swamp when a partially submerged log is hit by lightning—is one such counterexample, according to some philosophers. Chapter 6 presents replies both to the Inverted Earth example and to Swampman.

Part III of the book deals with two more general issues, one of which is potentially threatening to representationalism and the other of which representationalism enables us to make progress upon. The potential threat is posed by color (and other so-called "secondary qualities"). For reasons that will become clear in chapters 3–6, representationalism of the sort I endorse requires an objectivist account of color. It does not require that colors be *external*, objective entities, but this is certainly the view of color that goes most naturally with representationalism. This is also, I believe, the commonsense view of color. Unfortunately, according to many color scientists and some philosophers, colors cannot be objective entities of the sort common sense supposes. Common sense supposedly conflicts with modern science on color, and common sense supposedly has no way of accommodating the distinction between unitary and binary colors. I argue that this is quite wrong. Chapter 7 may thus be seen as a vindication of common sense and thereby indirectly a defense of representationalism with respect to color.

The final chapter considers an important question about consciousness on which philosophers have been largely silent, namely: Where, on the phylogenetic scale, does phenomenal consciousness cease? I address this question from the perspective of representationalism, and I argue that consciousness extends beyond the realm of vertebrates to such simple creatures as honey bees.

I have given talks at many places on the essays that comprise this book, and I am indebted to many people for helpful comments, discussion, and/or correspondence. In particular, I would like to thank the Department of Philosophy at the University of Bielefeld for hosting a week-long seminar on Tye 1995 (during which I was asked a large number of useful and probing questions) as well as the following individuals: Kent Bach, Ansgar Beckermann, Ned Block, David Chalmers, Earl Conee, Martin Davies, Fred Dretske, John Dilworth, Jim Edwards, Frank Hofmann, Terry Horgan, Keith Hossack, Frank Jackson, Joe Levine, David Lewis, Peter Ludlow, Colin McGinn, Brian McLaughlin, Christian Nimtz, John O'Leary Hawthorne, Andrew Melnyk, Tom Nagel, Chris Peacocke, David Papineau, Jesse Prinz, Diana Rafmann, Alex Rosenberg, Mark Sainsbury, David Sanford, Krista Saporiti, Giofranco Soldati, Wade Savage, Sydney Shoemaker, Eilrt Sundt-Ohlsen, Bernhard Thole, and Bob Van Gulick.

Some of the essays are entirely new; others involve a significant reworking of previously published articles. Chapter 1 differs only very minimally from an essay with the same title that appeared in German in an issue of *Protosociologie* (1998), edited by K. Preier. Chapter 2 appeared in *Mind* (October 1999) as "Phenomenal Consciousness: The Explanatory Gap as a Cognitive Illusion." An ancestor of chapter 6 was published as "Inverted Earth, Swampman, and Representationism" in *Philosophical Perspectives* (1998), but the latter part of the chapter that appears here is notably different from the earlier essay. Chapter 8 is taken from the last two-thirds of an article with the same title that appeared in *Philosophical Studies* (1997).

Notes

1. It is sometimes held that the content of a conscious thought makes its own distinctive contribution to the phenomenal character of a thinker's mental state. This has the very counterintuitive consequence that my molecular duplicate on Putnam's famous planet, Twin Earth, who thinks that twin water (or twater) is wet, rather than that water is wet, *thereby* differs from me at the level of phenomenal experience or feeling. I accept, of course, that what my twin thinks is different from me. He has a thought with a different content from mine, and if he is conscious of what is thinking then his thought has a different conscious

content. But this is not a difference in *phenomenal* consciousness, at least in any sense that I intend. The difference, rather, is one of *higher-order* consciousness. He believes that he is thinking that twater is wet whereas I believe that I am thinking that water is wet.

2. I do not wish to deny that attending to a sensory experience can sometimes *causally* influence its phenomenal character. For more on attention and phenomenal consciousness, see chapter 1, pp. 13–14; also chapter 3, pp. 60–61.

I

Challenges to Reductive Theories of Consciousness

1
Knowing What It Is Like: The Ability Hypothesis and the Knowledge Argument

Mary, as the familiar story goes (Jackson 1982), is imprisoned in a black and white room. Never having been permitted to leave it, she acquires information about the world outside from the black and white books her captors have made available to her, from the black and white television sets attached to external cameras, and from the black and white monitor screens hooked up to banks of computers. As time passes, Mary acquires more and more information about the physical aspects of color and color vision. She comes to know all the familiar color names and the objects to which they apply, the physical character of the surfaces of those objects, the way the light is reflected, the changes in the retina and the optic nerve as different colors are perceived, the physical changes in the visual cortex. Eventually, she becomes the world's leading authority on color and color vision. Indeed she comes to know *all* the physical facts pertinent to everday colors and color vision.

Still, as the years go by, she becomes more and more dissatisfied. She wonders to herself: What do people in the outside world *experience* when they see the various colors? *What is it like* for them to see red or green? No matter how often she reads her books or how long she spends examining the printouts from her computers, she still can't answer these questions fully.[1] One day her captors release her. She is free at last to see things with their real colors (and free too to scrub off the awful black and white paint that covers her body). She steps outside her room into a garden full of flowers. "So, that is what it is like to experience red," she exclaims, as she sees a red rose. "And that," she adds, looking down at the grass, "is what it is like to experience green."

Mary here seems to make some important discoveries. She seems to find out things she did not know before. How can that be, if, as seems possible at least in principle, she has all the physical information there is to have about color and color vision—that is, if she knows all the pertinent physical facts?

One popular explanation among philosophers (so-called "qualia freaks") is that that there is a realm of subjective, phenomenal qualities associated with color, qualities the intrinsic nature of which Mary comes to discover upon her release, as she herself undergoes the various new color experiences. Before she left her room, she only knew the objective, physical basis of those subjective qualities, their causes and effects, and various relations of similarity and difference. She had no knowledge of the subjective qualities in themselves.

This explanation is not available to the physicalist. If what it is like for someone to experience red is one and the same as some physical quality, then Mary already knows *that* while in her room. Likewise, for experiences of the other colors. For Mary knows all the pertinent physical facts. What, then, can the physicalist say?

Some physicalists respond that knowing what it is like is know-how and nothing more. Mary acquires certain abilities—for example, the ability to recognize red things by sight alone, the ability to imagine a green expanse. She does *not* come to know any new information, any new facts about color, any new qualities. This is the view of David Lewis. In the postscript to "Mad Pain and Martian Pain," he comments:

... knowing what it is like isn't the possession of information at all. It isn't the elimination of any hitherto open possibilities. Rather, knowing what it is like is the possession of abilities: abilities to recognize, abilities to imagine, abilities to predict one's behavior by imaginative experiments (1983, p. 131).

In a similar vein, in his essay "What Experience Teaches," Lewis says:

The Ability Hypothesis says that knowing what an experience is like just *is* the possession of these abilities to remember, imagine, and recognize. . . . It isn't knowing-that. It's knowing-how. (1990, p. 516)

Lawrence Nemirow holds the same (or almost the same) view:

Knowing what an experience is like is the same as knowing how to imagine having the experience. (1990, p. 495)

Is the Ability Hypothesis true? Moreover, if it is true, is it really the case that captive Mary poses no problem for physicalism? In what follows, I argue that the answer to both of these questions is "No." I also propose an alternative hybrid account of knowing what it is like that ties it conceptually both to knowing-that and to knowing-how. Given this account, I maintain, the physicalist still has a satisfactory response to the case of Mary and the Knowledge Argument.[2]

1.1   The Hypothesis Clarified

Lewis identifies knowing what an experience is like with certain abilities. What exactly are these abilities supposed to be? To begin with, there is the ability to remember the experience in question. Suppose you smell a skunk for the first time, and you thereby learn what it is like to smell a skunk. Afterward, you can remember the experience. Moreover, by remembering it, you can imaginatively recreate it. This will be the case, even if, as Lewis notes, you eventually forget the occasion on which you had the experience. By having the experience of smelling a skunk, you gain new abilities to remember and imagine.

Included within the ability to imagine is more than just the ability to imagine the experience you underwent earlier. After seeing something red, for example, and seeing something yellow, you are able to imagine something red with yellow spots, even if you have never seen anything red with yellow spots. By imagining certain situations you could not imagine before, you also gain the ability to predict with a fair degree of confidence what you would do were the situations to arise. For example, having seen the color purple, you can now imagine how you would likely react if you were offered a purple shirt to wear.

Another important ability you gain is the ability to recognize the experience when it comes again. Lewis says:

If you taste Vegemite on another day [your second encounter with it], you will probably know that you have met the taste once before. And if, while tasting Vegemite, you know that it is Vegemite that you are tasting, then you will be able to put the name to the experience if you have it again. (1990, p. 515)

These abilities—to remember, imagine, and recognize—constitute knowing what it is like, in Lewis view. There is no claim that you *could* not possibly have these abilities without having the relevant experiences. After all, you might acquire them by some possible future neurophysiology or by magic. The point is that, given how the world actually works, lessons alone won't do the trick, no matter how complicated they become. Experience, as Lewis puts it, is the best teacher about what a new experience is like.

1.2   The Three L's (Levin, Lycan, and Loar): Some Unpersuasive Objections to the Ability Hypothesis

Janet Levin suggests that the Ability Hypothesis has a number of undesirable consequences. She comments:

First of all, it would be perverse to claim that bare experience can provide us only with practical abilities. . . . By being shown an unfamilar color, I acquire information about its similarities and compatibilities with other colors, and its effects on other of our mental states: surely I seem to be acquiring certain facts about that color and the visual experience of it. (1990, p. 479)

This seems to me to miss the point. It is certainly true that *I* can gain information about a color I have never seen before by experiencing it. The real question, however, is whether Mary could or whether I could in a comparable situation. In actual fact, I myself do not know all the relevant physical facts; so, of course, *I* can learn things about similarities and differences and causes and effects by undergoing new color experiences. Mary's situation is different, however. Arguably, she already knows all such relations for the case of color even though she does not know what it is like to experience the various colors. As Lewis observes,

Maybe Mary knows enough to triangulate each color experience exactly in a network of resemblances, or in many networks of resemblance in different respects, while never knowing what any node of any network is like. (1990, p. 502)

The Ability Hypothesis has it that Mary's failure to know what any node in any network is like consists in her lacking certain crucial abilities. Nothing in Levin's first objection undercuts this claim.

Levin has a second objection:

. . . it is not implausible to suppose that experience is the *only* source of at least some of these facts. . . . [H]ow *does* one convey the taste of pineapple to someone who has not yet tried it, and does that first taste not dramatically increase, if not fully constitute, the knowledge of what the taste of pineapple is?

Again, this seems uncompelling. The first taste of pineapple provides one with knowledge of what the taste of pineapple is like, as everyone agrees. In Lewis's view (1990, p. 519), the expression "what experience E is like" denotes experience E. So, Lewis can happily grant that knowledge of what the taste of pineapple is like is knowledge of the taste of pineapple, of what that taste is.[3] The real issue concerns the *kind* of knowledge acquired here. Lewis says that it is knowledge-how. Having tasted pineapple, one has the ability to remember what the taste of pineapple is, to imagine the taste, and so on. Levin evidently takes the opposing view. But she has not given us a clear reason in her second objection for taking her side.

Levin's final objection follows:

. . . there seem to be important cognitive differences between ourselves and those incapable of sharing our experiences. It would seem extremely natural to explain this by appeal to differences in our knowledge of the facts about experience: indeed what other explanation could there be? (1990, p. 479)

The obvious reply by the advocate of the Ability Hypothesis is that the difference can be explained by differences in cognitive abilities. If you have never experienced a certain experience E, you lack the ability to remember E, to recognize E when it comes again, to imagine E.

All of the above objections by Levin to the Ability Hypothesis are endorsed by Lycan (1996). He has some further objections of his own, none of which seems to me very persuasive. I shall briefly discuss four.

Lycan tells us that instances of "S knows wh- . . ." are closely related to "S knows that . . ." For example, "I know where Tom is" is true by virtue of my knowing that Tom is in such-and-such place. Likewise, "You know who Bill Clinton is" is true by virtue of your knowing that Bill Clinton is so-and-so (e.g., the president of the United States). This model leads Lycan to propose that "S knows what it is like to see blue" means (roughly): "S knows that it is like Q to see blue," where 'Q' names the pertinent phenomenal quality. So, according to Lycan, the "knowing what it is like" locution does not pick out an ability at all.

Presumably Lycan introduces the name 'Q' into the proposed analysis rather than an indexical for a phenomenal quality, since one can know what it is like to experience blue at times at which one is not experiencing it and hence at times at which one does not know that experiencing blue is like *this*. But the presence of a qualia name within a propositional attitude context creates a difficulty. If I can know that Hesperus is a planet without knowing that Phosphorus is a planet, even though 'Hesperus' and 'Phosphorus' are coreferential, I can surely likewise know that seeing blue is like *Q* without knowing that seeing blue is like *R*, or vice versa, even though '*Q*' and '*R*' denote the same phenomenal quality. So, which name is the appropriate one for the analysis? Presumably whichever name *S* antecedently knows or introduces for the relevant phenomenal quality. Still, what if *S* neither introduces a name nor knows one already? This surely does not preclude *S* from knowing what it is like to see blue. Moreover, even if *S* has a suitable name, she can satisfy Lycan's analysans without satisfying the analysandum.

Consider again Mary. Arguably, as Lewis suggests, Mary knows enough to triangulate each color experience within a network of resemblances. Hence, she knows of the experience of indigo, for example, that it is like seeing blue. If she names the former experience '*Q*', Mary knows that seeing blue is like *Q*. However, Mary does not know what it is like to see blue (or indigo) until she leaves her cell. This objection, I might add, also refutes the suggestion that "*S* knows what it is like to see blue" means "There is a phenomenal quality (or state) such that *S* knows that seeing blue is like it."

So Lycan has not shown that "knowing what it's like" sentences are analyzable as "knowing-that" sentences. Nor is it obvious how to revise Lycan's proposal satisfactorily.

A rather different objection Lycan raises is that comparisons can be made between what it is like to experience one thing (e.g., hydrogen sulphide) and what it is like to experience another (e.g., rotten eggs). What it's like, then, is a matter of fact. "The facts in question per se are not about imagining but about actually smelling," Lycan asserts, "[a]nd what is factual is propositional" (1996, p. 99).

It seems to me that Lewis would deny none of this. He explicitly allows that color experiences can be compared, and also that what it is like to taste Vegemite can be compared to what it is like to taste Marmite (Lewis, 1990, pp. 501–2). He explicitly asserts that what experience *E* is like is the same as *E*. So, what it's like, according to Lewis, is a matter of fact. The issue, to repeat what I said earlier, concerns *knowledge* of what it's like. Lycan's argument for the conclusion that the relevant knowledge is propositional is a nonsequitur.[4]

Lycan has another objection from success or failure. If knowing what it is like to experience red is largely being able to imagine experiencing red, the imagining here must be accurate. I do not know what it is like to experience red, if, when I take myself to be imagining it, I am really visualizing blue. From this, Lycan concludes:

. . . there is such a thing as getting "what it's like" right, representing truly rather than falsely, from which it seems to follow that "knowing what it's like" is knowing a truth. (1990, p. 99)

This is a blatant non sequitur. From the fact that the abilities with which knowing what it is like is identified are abilities to be in certain propositional states, it certainly does *not* follow that knowing what it is like is knowing a truth. What follows is that knowing what it's like consists in abilities, the exercise of which demands (at the time of exercise) the representation of certain truths. So what?

Lycan also objects that the Ability Hypothesis leaves us without a satisfactory explanation of why we have the abilities it describes. Consider our ability to visualize red. How is this best explained? According to Lycan, the answer is that we have factual knowledge of what it is like to experience red. No such explanation is available to Lewis.

This again seems to me inconclusive. Lewis can respond that we have the ability to visualize red because we have experienced red, and we can generate a mental image of red from a suitable memory representation of the experience. Of course, the ability to generate images from memory representations itself needs some sort of explanation. However, this explanation (which lies within the domain of cognitive science) is not obviously one that need appeal to factual knowledge of what it is like to see red. For it is not at all obvious that the relevant memory representations will be propositional at all. One alternative possibility is that they are stored representations with a picture-like format.[5]

The third objector to the Ability Hypothesis, Brian Loar (1990), cites two objections. His initial complaint (echoed again by Lycan, 1996) is as follows:

One can have knowledge not only of the form "pains feel like such and such" but also of the form "*if* pains feel like such and such then Q". Perhaps you could get away with saying that the former expresses (not a genuine judgement but) the mere possession of recognitional know-how. There seems however no comparable way of accounting for the embedded occurrence of 'feels like such and such' in the latter; it seems to introduce a predicate with a distinct content. (1990, p. 96)

It is not easy to evaluate this objection since Lewis and Nemirow focus on the locution "knows what it is like," not the locution "feels like such and such." Their claim is simply that the former expresses an ability. Still, let us take a concrete example: Suppose I have never felt any pains before, and I remark about my current experience (P): "If pains feel like *this*, then I do not want to feel pain ever again." As noted earlier, Lewis claims that "what experience E is like" denotes E. So, in Lewis's view, (P) may be recast as simply "If this is pain, then I do not want to experience it again."[6]

What is supposed to be the problem here? No one who endorses the Ability Hypothesis should deny that the final quoted sentence expresses a genuine judgment. Lewis, for example, is a realist about pain. Pain, in his view, is both a brain state and a functional state (1983a). Abilities enter only with respect to *knowing what pain is like*. One's knowledge of the state of pain, when one knows what it is like, consists in the possession of certain cognitive abilities, all of which pertain to that state (e.g., the ability to recognize *it* when it comes again, the ability to imagine *it*, and so forth).

So far so good, then, for the Ability Hypothesis. But Loar has one further objection:

For many conceptions of phenomenal qualities, there simply is no candidate for an independently mastered term, instances of which one then proceeds to learn how to recognize: my conception of a peculiar way my left knee feels when I run (a conception that occurs predicatively in various judgments) is not my knowing how to apply an independently mastered predicate. (1990, p. 86)

The obvious riposte is: Whoever said that the conceptions pertinent to the relevant abilities must be ones that correlate neatly with linguistic terms? If I know the way my left knee feels when I run, then, according to the Ability Theorist, I must have certain abilities. These abilities (to recognize, to imagine) require conceptions. But the conceptions need not be ones that their subjects can articulate publicly in language. Of course, if Loar here has in mind terms in the language of thought, then this response is inappropriate. But Loar's initial claim now needs defense. For why should the Ability Theorist accept that there are no suitable terms in the language of thought, terms that are deployed when the pertinent abilities are exercised?

Still, there is, I believe, a real difficulty lurking here in the background for the Ability Hypothesis. It is to the development of this difficulty that I turn in the next section.

1.3   The Problem as I See It

Human sensory experience is enormously rich. Take color experience. There is a plenitude of detail here that goes far beyond our concepts. Humans can experience an enormous number of subtly different colors, something on the order of 10 million, according to some estimates. But we have names for only a few of these colors, and we also have no stored representations in memory for most colors. There simply isn't enough room. My experience of red_{19}, for example, is phenomenally different from my experience of red_{21}, even though I have no stored memory representations of these specific hues and hence no such concepts as the concepts red_{19} and red_{21}. This is why I cannot go into a paint store and reliably identify a color on a chart as *exactly* matching the precise hue of my dining room walls. I possess the concept *red*, of course, and I exercise it when I recognize something as red, but I lack the concepts for determinate hues. My ordinary color judgments are, of necessity, far less discriminating than my experiences of color. Human memory simply isn't up to the task of capturing the wealth of detail found in the experiences. Beliefs or judgments abstract from the details and impose more general categories. Sensory experience is the basis for many beliefs or judgments, but it is far, far richer.

This point is not restricted to color, of course. The same is true for our sensory experiences of sounds, to mention another obvious example. They, too, admit of many more fine-grained distinctions than our stored representations of sounds in memory. Experiences of shapes are likewise nonconceptual. Presented with an inkblot, for example, Mary will likely have an experience of a shape for which she has no corresponding concept.[7]

When Mary first sees the rose and exclaims, "So, that is what it is like to see red," she certainly acquires certain abilities, as Lewis and Nemirow suppose. She is now able to recognize red things by sight; she can identify the experience of red when it comes again; afterward, she can remember the experience of red; she can imagine what it is for something to be red. So far no obvious difficulty. But she knows more than just what it is like to experience red. As she stares at the rose, it is also true of her at that time that she knows what it is like to experience the particular determinate hue of red—call it 'red$_{17}$'—she is seeing. Of course, she does not know that hue *as* red$_{17}$. Her conception of it is indexical; she thinks of it only as *that* shade of red. But she certainly knows what it is like to experience that particular hue *at the time at which she is experiencing it.*

What is the new ability that Mary acquires here? She is not now able to recognize things that are red$_{17}$ as red$_{17}$ by sight. Ex hypothesi, Mary is one of us, a human being. She lacks the concept *red$_{17}$*. Nor is she able to recognize things other than the rose as having that very determinate color (whatever it is). She has no mental template that is sufficiently fine-grained to permit her to identify the experience of red$_{17}$ when it comes again. Presented with two items (one red$_{17}$ and the other red$_{18}$) in a series of tests, she cannot say with any accuracy which experience her earlier experience of the rose matches. Sometimes she picks one; at other times she picks the other. Nor is she able afterward to imagine things as having hue, red$_{17}$, or as having that very shade of red the rose had; and for precisely the same reason.

Mary lacks the abilities Lewis lists. But, as she stares at the rose, she certainly knows what it is like to experience the particular shade of red she is experiencing. If you doubt this, suppose we inform Mary that she is seeing red$_{17}$. She replies, "So, this is what it is like to see red$_{17}$. I had always wondered. Seventeen, you see, is my favorite number; and red the color of my mother's favorite dress." We then say to her, "No, you don't know what it is like to see red$_{17}$. For you won't remember it accurately when you take your eyes from the rose; you won't be able to recognize it when it comes again; you won't be able to imagine the experience of seeing red$_{17}$." Should Mary then admit that she doesn't really know what it is like to see red$_{17}$ even while she is staring at the rose? She won't know it later certainly. But it seems intuitively bizarre to deny that she knows it *at the time.*

Perhaps it is correct to say that Mary never really *learns* what it is like to see red$_{17}$, for learning arguably requires not just knowledge but the retention of that knowledge. You haven't learned that the distance of the earth from the sun is 93 million miles if you only know it at the moment your teacher tells you. You need to retain that knowledge to have genuinely learned what the distance is. But the Knowledge Argument against physicalism is just that: an argument from knowledge. It makes no essential use of the concept of learning. The main claim is that Mary comes to *know* things she didn't know before even though she knows all the physical facts.

I conclude that the Ability Hypothesis, as elaborated by Lewis, does not afford us a satisfactory *general* account of knowing what it is like. The Knowledge Argument still presents physicalism with a very serious difficulty.

1.4   A Possible Revision to the Ability Hypothesis

When Mary leaves her room, she gains certain abilities. Among them is the ability to recognize certain experiences when they come again. Another more basic ability is the ability to *cognize* the experience for as long as it is present. The latter ability, it might be said, is one Mary possesses even with respect to the experience of red$_{17}$. For when Mary first sees that particular shade of red, she does have the ability then and there to cognize her experience as an experience with *that* phenomenal character. Perhaps knowing what it is like should be identified not with the cluster of abilities Lewis cites—for they may all be lacking while knowing what it is like is present—but rather with the more basic ability to apply an indexical concept to the phenomenal character of her experience via introspection.

This, it seems to me, still won't save the Ability Hypothesis. Mary, when she is shown the rose for the first time, may be distracted. Perhaps she is still thinking hard about a theoretical problem that occupied her in her black and white room. The fact that she is distracted does not entail that she doesn't undergo any color experience any more than the fact that I am sometimes distracted by philosophical thoughts when I drive entails that I no longer see the road and the cars ahead. I am able at such times to attend to my visual sensations even though I do not do so. But the visual sensations are there all right. How else do I keep the car on the road? And the same points apply *mutatis mutandis* to Mary. She has her eyes open. The rose is immediately before her. She is not cognitively blocked from her visual experiences by a psychological impairment. She *can* introspect those experiences even if, in fact, she does not do so.

Now if Mary sees the rose, as I see the road ahead in the driving example, then she must have a visual experience caused by it. If, say, she has massive damage to the visual cortex, then it won't matter what activity the rose elicits in the cells of her retina: she won't have any visual experiences and she won't *see* anything.[8] But if Mary has visual *experiences*, then she must have consciousness at the phenomenal level. There must be something it is like for her as she sees the rose. Her state must have a certain phenomenal character. What it is like for her is something she can become aware of by introspection. Had she paid attention to her visual state, she would have been conscious of it in the higher-order sense. She would have formed a thought about it. She would have been aware that she was undergoing that visual experience. But, in fact, Mary is distracted. And being distracted, she does not actually apply *any* concept at all to her experience. In these circumstances, she clearly does not know what it is like to have the experience in question. For she has no conception, no cognitive awareness of her phenomenal state. But she certainly has the *ability* to mentally point to the phenomenal character of her experience with an indexical concept via introspection. So, here the proposed ability is present, but knowing what it is like is absent. In the earlier examples, the reverse had been true. Cut the pie, any way you like, then, the Ability Hypothesis is false.

Of course, I am not claiming that knowing what it is like is never the possession of abilities. In particular, I am not claiming that in those cases where the subject has the appropriate concept knowing what it is like is not the possession of abilities. Nothing that I have said undercuts the claim that knowing what it is like to experience red, for example, is a cluster of abilities of the sort Lewis proposes. But the 'is' here cannot be the 'is' of identity. Knowing what it is like to experience red and knowing what it is like to experience red_{17} have something in common: they are both cases of knowing what it is like. This common feature is lost if knowing what it is like to experience red is literally one and the same as the possession of certain abilities.

It is also worth stressing that even if some specimens of knowing what it is like could be identified with various abilities, this would not help the physicalist with the Knowledge Argument. For if there are *any* examples of knowing what it is like that do not conform to some version of the Ability Hypothesis, then physicalism is threatened. And that there are such examples is what I have been primarily at pains to show.

I now want to make the case for something stronger: that physicalism is threatened by the Knowledge Argument, even if knowing what is is like *is* an ability or cluster of abilities. If this is correct, then the Ability Hypothesis has less significance than is usually supposed. Consider again Mary as she remarks, "So, this is what it is like to experience red." Intuitively, in making this remark, Mary is expressing a discovery that she has made. But what has she discovered? Well, she now knows what it is like to experience red. So, on the Ability Hypothesis, she has acquired some know-how. But that know-how she retains even after she stops having any experience of red; and intuitively, there is a cognitive difference between Mary at the time at which she makes her remark and Mary later on, after the experience ceases (at least at those times at which she is not exercising any of the pertinent abilities). If we agree with Lewis that what experience E is like is the same as E, then the difference seems well captured by saying that while she is attending to her experience, Mary has knowledge-that she didn't have before, knowledge (in part) that this is the experience of red.[9] Moreover, even if we distinguish what experience E is like from E, we can still say that Mary has knowledge-that she didn't have before, namely, knowledge that this is the phenomenal character of the experience of red. So, either way, Mary does make a genuine propositional discovery. And that, according to advocates of the Knowledge Argument, spells trouble for physicalism.

1.5   More on Knowing What It Is Like and the Knowledge Argument

In the case described in the section above in which Mary is distracted, Mary has knowledge of how to do something. She knows how to mentally point to the phenomenal character of her experience in introspection. But, being distracted, she doesn't exercise her know-how. Were she to do so, she would turn her knowledge-how into knowledge-that. Intuitively, she would come to know that *that* is the phenomenal character of her experience. And in so doing, she would come to know what it is like to have an experience of that sort. So, introspective knowing-that is sufficient for knowing what it is like. Such knowing-that is not necessary, however. One need not be paying attention to one's current experiences to know what it is like to experience red. Intuitively, in such a case, it is necessary and sufficient to have abilities of the sort Lewis describes. It seems, then, that knowing what it is like is best captured by a disjunction of introspective knowing-that and knowing-how along the following lines:

S knows what it is like to undergo experience *E* = df Either *S* is now undergoing *E*, and *S* has knowledge-that with respect to the phenomenal character of *E* obtained via current introspection, or *S* has the Lewis abilities with respect to *E*.

This proposal is similar to one I made some years ago (Tye, 1986), and it still seems to me to do more justice to our ordinary understanding of the expression "know what it is like" than does any other I have seen. But prima facie it leaves the physicalist with a problem. For how can it now be denied that Mary gains some new propositional knowledge when she leaves her room as she introspects her new experiences—for example, knowledge that this is the experience of red, while viewing a ripe tomato; or knowledge, on the same occasion, that she is having an experience of this phenomenal type? The worry, of course, is that physicalism cannot allow such discoveries.

Let us focus first on Mary's discovery that this is the experience of red. It will not suffice for the physicalist to try to explain this discovery by saying simply that, confined to her cell, Mary can form no indexical conception of the experience of red or any particular shade of red. For if the experience of red is a physical state, then it is not at all obvious that captive Mary cannot perceptually demonstrate it, as it is tokened in others outside her room—given the appropriate finely focused, high-tech, viewing apparatus.

A more promising strategy is to argue that Mary, while she is confined, lacks the phenomenal concept *red*.[10] This is not to say that she attaches no meaning to the term 'red'. On the contrary, given the information at her disposal, she can use the term correctly in a wide range of cases. Still, the concept Mary exercises here is nonphenomenal. She does not know what it is like to experience red; and intuitively knowing what it is like to have that experience is necessary for possession of the phenomenal concept *red*.[11] It follows that there is a thought that Mary cannot think to herself while in her room, namely the thought *that this is the experience of red*, where the concept *red*, as it is exercised in this thought, is the one she acquires upon her release after seeing red things. But if she cannot think this thought as she languishes in her cell, she cannot know its content then. Since she does know that content upon her release, she discovers something. Experience is her teacher even though, according to the physicalist, there is nothing nonphysical in the world that makes her new thought true.

Perhaps it will be replied that if Mary acquires various phenomenal concepts pertaining to color experience upon her release, then she cannot really know all there is to know about the nature of color vision from within her room; for where a difference between the old and the new concepts obtains, a difference in the world between the properties these concepts stand for or express must also obtain. Some of these properties she knew in her cell; others she became cognizant of only upon her release. That I simply deny, however. Properties individuate no more finely than causal powers, but conceptual differences exist even between concepts that are analytically equivalent. So, conceptual differences need not be mirrored in worldly differences. Sense is one thing, reference another.[12]

Consider now Mary's thought *that she is having an experience with this phenomenal character*, as she introspects her first experience of red. Here it is certainly the case that she cannot think this thought truly, while she is held in her room. For the concept *this*, exercised in her thought, refers to the phenomenal character associated with her experiencing red and Mary, in her room, never experiences red. So, once again, when she thinks a thought of this sort on the appropriate occasion, she is making a genuine discovery.

The position sketched above assumes that demonstrative thoughts and thought-contents are partly individuated by the item picked out by the demonstrative and partly by the various general concepts and associated modes of presentation exercised in the thoughts. That real-world items play a role in individuating indexical thoughts and thought contents is an externalist claim that is very widely accepted, and one which needs no further argument here. That concepts and modes of presentation are also involved in the individuation of thought-contents should also be uncontroversial, given one sense of the term *content*—the sense in which thought-content is whatever information that-clauses provide that suffices for the purposes of even the most demanding rationalizing explanation. In this sense, what I think, when I think that Cicero was an orator, is not what I think when I think that Tully was an orator. This is precisely why it is possible to discover that Cicero is Tully. The thought that Cicero was an orator differs from the thought that Tully was an orator not at the level of truth-conditions—the same singular proposition is partly constitutive of the content of both—but at the level of concepts and modes of presentation. The one thought exercises the concept *Cicero*; the other the concept *Tully*. The concepts have the same reference; but because they present the referent in different ways, the two thoughts can play different roles in rationalizing explanation.

So, there is no difficulty in holding that Mary comes to know some new things upon her release, while already knowing all the pertinent real-world physical facts, even though the new experiences she undergoes and their introspectible qualities are wholly physical.[13] In an ordinary, everyday sense, Mary's knowledge increases. And that is all the physicalist needs to answer the Knowledge Argument.

Some philosophers (including Lewis) individuate thought contents more coarsely than I have above, as, for example, sets of possible worlds. On this view, the thought that $7 + 5 = 12$ has the very same content as the thought that all bachelors are unmarried. However, it seems intuitively undeniable that the event type, thinking that $7 + 5 = 12$, plays a different role in rationalizing explanation than the event type, thinking that all bachelors are unmarried. So, on this approach, thought-types cannot be individuated for the purposes of rationalizing explanations by their contents alone. Two different thought types can have the same content. Likewise for belief types.

It follows that even on this two-factor theory of thought-types (according to which thought-types are individuated by their contents plus some other factor), the physicalist can insist that there is a perfectly good sense in which Mary discovers that so-and-so is the case after she is released. For she comes to instantiate cognitive thought-types (knowing-that types) she did not instantiate before, even though, given her exhaustive knowledge of the physical facts, the contents of her thought-types before and after remain unchanged. And if Mary or anyone else knows that p at time t without knowing that p before t, then surely it is correct to say, in ordinary parlance, that the person has made a discovery at t.

My overall conclusion is that there is much that is right in the Ability Hypothesis, but that it cannot be the whole truth about the nature of knowing what it is like. Moreover, even if it were the whole truth, there would still be propositional cases of knowing, not themselves properly classifiable as knowing what it is like, that advocates of the Knowledge Argument might well take to refute physicalism. This should not overly concern the physicalist, however. Even with the demise of the Ability Hypothesis, these cases can be comfortably handled in the manner I have indicated. Either way, then, the Knowledge Argument can be answered.

Notes

1. For a real life case of a visual scientist (Knut Norby) who is an achromotope, see Sacks (1996, chapter 1).

2. Of course, the case of Mary is a threat not only to physicalism with respect to phenomenal qualities but also to functionalism: Mary has all the pertinent functional information, too. To simplify exposition, I focus on physicalism. But what I say applies *mutatis mutandis* to functionalism.

3. Nemirow (1990) takes a different view. His claim is that "what E is like" is a syncategorematic part of the expression "know what experience E is like." This creates difficulties for him of a sort that Lewis can avoid.

4. A response of the same sort can be given to Lycan's argument from attempting-to-describe (1996, p. 98).

5. See, for example, Kosslyn (1980). These representations (in Kosslyn's view) are also importantly dissimilar from pictures.

6. For Lewis, pain and the feeling of pain are one and the same (Lewis, 1983, p. 130).

7. For more on this topic, see chapters 3 and 4.

8. I ignore here blindsight. My remark is made with respect to normal, every-day seeing.

9. By parallel reasoning, we may infer that Mary has other new knowledge-that associated with her experience of red, notably knowledge that she is having an experience of this particular shade of red and knowledge that she is having an experience of this phenomenal type. The latter knowledge, incidentally, should be granted even by those who deny that what experience E is like is the same as E.

10. Those who take the view that inversion scenarios show that no phenomenal character need be shared by all actual and possible tokens of the experience of red will want to deny that Mary discovers *that this is the experience of red* and, correspondingly, that there is any such concept as the *phenomenal* concept *red*. This position is compatible with holding that Mary nonetheless makes some discoveries as she introspects her first experience of red: for example, *that this is R*, where the concept R is a phenomenal concept of the phenomenal character associated with the experience of red in Mary, and *that I am having an experience with this phenomenal character*. The concept R is one Mary lacks in her room. For a discussion of the latter discovery, see below, pp. 17–18. The former discovery may be handled in a way parallel to that given in the text for the discovery that this is the experience of red.

11. Phenomenal concepts are discussed in detail in chapter 2.

12. For more here, see chapter 2.

13. The term 'fact' is itself ambiguous. Sometimes it is used to pick out real-world states of affairs alone; sometimes it is used for such states of affairs under certain conceptualizations. When I speak of the physical facts here, I refer either to physical states of affairs alone or to those states of affairs under purely physical conceptualizations. (For more on 'fact', see Tye 1995.)

2

The Explanatory Gap as a Cognitive Illusion

Woody Allen once remarked, "What a wonderful thing, to be conscious! I wonder what the people of New Jersey do?" However things are in New Jersey, what is wonderful about consciousness, or at least most immediately striking, is the subjective or phenomenal character of such states as the visual experience of bright red, the feeling of elation, the sensation of being tickled. Our grasp of what it is like to undergo these and other experiential states is supplied to us by introspection. We also have an admittedly incomplete grasp of what goes on objectively in the brain and the body. But there is, it seems, a vast chasm between the two. Presented with the current physical and functional story of the objective changes that occur when such-and-such subjective feelings are experienced, we have the strong sense that the former does not fully explain the latter, that the phenomenology has been left out. We naturally ask: What is so special about *those* physical or functional goings-on? Why do they feel like *that*? Indeed, why do they feel any way at all?

Compare this case with that of solidity or digestion, say. Once one learns that in solid things the molecules are not free to move around as they are in liquids, one immediately grasps that solid things do not pour easily, that they tend to retain their shape and volume. Having been told the physical story, to ask: "Yes, but why are things with molecules that are fixed in place solid? Why shouldn't such things not be solid?" is to show a conceptual confusion. One who responds in this way simply does not understood the ordinary notion of solidity. What it is for something to be solid is for it to be disposed to retain its shape and volume (roughly). Once the molecules are fixed, the shape and volume are fixed and thereby, automatically, the disposition to retain shape and volume, that is, the solidity.

Similar points apply in the case of digestion. Upon learning that enzymes in the alimentary canals of human beings break down food and convert it into energy, only a failure to grasp that the word "digestion" means (roughly) *internal process whose function is to convert food into energy* could lead one to ask: "Why does the action of these enzymes in humans generate digestion? Why shouldn't the enzymes turn food into energy in the absence of digestion?"

In the case of phenomenal consciousness, however, the corresponding questions remain even for those who understand full well the relevant phenomenal terms and who know the underlying physical and functional story. One who has a complete understanding of the term 'pain', for example, and who is fully apprised of the physical facts as we now know them, can still coherently ask why such-and-such brain processes or functional states feel the way pains do or why these processes feel any way at all. In this case, it seems that as far as our understanding goes, *something important is missing*. Herein lies the famous "explanatory gap" for consciousness.[1]

Some say that the explanatory gap is unbridgable and that the proper conclusion to draw from it is that there is a corresponding gap in the world. Experiences and feelings have irreducibly subjective, nonphysical qualities over and above whatever physical qualities they have. The physical (and functional) story is incomplete (*qualophilia*: Jackson 1982, 1993; Chalmers 1996). Others take essentially the same position on the gap while urging that being objective is not a necessary condition of being physical. Thus, it is claimed, there is nothing in the gap that detracts from a purely physicalist view of experiences and feelings. The introspectible, phenomenal qualities of experiences and feelings are indeed irreducibly subjective, but this is compatible with their being physical (*closet qualophilia*: Searle 1992). Others hold that the explanatory gap *may* one day be bridged but we currently lack the concepts to bring the subjective and objective perspectives together. On this view, it may turn out that phenomenal states are physical, but we currently have no clear conception as to how they could be (*physicalism, fingers crossed*: Nagel 1974). Still others adamantly insist that experiences and feelings are as much a part of the physical, natural world as life, photosynthesis, DNA, or lightning. It is just that with the concepts we have and the concepts we are capable of forming, we are cognitively closed to a full, bridging explanation by the very structure of our minds. There is such an explanation, but it is necessarily beyond our cognitive grasp (*physicalism, deeply pessimistic*: McGinn 1991).[2]

I reject all of these positions. What they have in common is the idea that if experiences are indeed fully physical, in the traditional sense of the term 'physical' (opposed by Searle), then an explanation is needed, but has not yet been found, for why the relevant physical states and qualities feel on the inside as they do. Where the proponents of these positions differ is over whether to affirm the antecedent of this conditional and thus to accept that the phenomenology of the appropriate physical entities needs explaining but is, as yet, unexplained or to deny that experiences are fully physical in the traditional sense, thereby removing the need for an explanation of the kind specified in the consequent. Jackson, Chalmers, and Searle do the latter; McGinn does the former, adding that the phenomenology will *never* be properly explained by us or by creatures like us. Nagel does not unequivocally fall into either camp, but overall he seems to favor the former strategy (without the thesis of cognitive closure).

I deny the conditional. I accept that experiences are fully, robustly physical but I maintain that there is no explanatory *gap* posed by their phenomenology.[3] The gap, I claim, is unreal; it is a cognitive illusion to which we only too easily fall prey. As such, it has no consequences for the nature of consciousness and physicalist or functionalist theories thereof. There is nothing in the alleged gap that should lead us to any bifurcation *in the world* between experiences and feelings, on the one hand, and physical or functional phenomena, on the other. There aren't two sorts of natural phenomena—the irreducibly subjective and the objective. The so-called "explanatory gap" derives largely from a failure to recognize the special features of phenomenal *concepts*. These concepts, I maintain, have a character that not only explains why we have the intuition that something important is left out by the physical (and/or functional) story but also explains why this intuition is not to be trusted.

My discussion is divided into four sections. I begin by making some remarks about the perspectival subjectivity of phenomenal states and I explain why I reject the familiar view that phenomenal concepts are simply indexical concepts that are applied to phenomenal states (see, e.g., Horgan 1984; Loar 1990; Rey 1991). In section 2.2, I go on to elaborate an account of phenomenal concepts. The nature of the alleged explanatory gap is addressed in section 2.3. Remaining worries are addressed in section 2.4.

2.1 Perspectival Subjectivity

One generally agreed-upon fact about phenomenal states is that they are perspectivally subjective. Consider the case of pain. It seems highly plausible to suppose that fully comprehending the character of the feeling of pain requires knowing what it is like to feel pain. And knowing what it is like to feel pain requires one to have a certain experiential point of view or perspective, namely the one conferred upon one by being the subject of pain. This is why a person born without the capacity to feel pain and kept alive in a very carefully controlled environment could never come to know what it is like to experience pain. Such a person could never herself adopt the relevant perspective. And lacking that perspective, she could never comprehend fully what that type of feeling was, no matter how much information was supplied about the firing patterns in the brains of people who are experiencing pain, the biochemical processes, the chemical changes, the disturbed bodily states.

Phenomenally conscious states, then, are perspectivally subjective in the following way: each phenomenal state S is such that fully comprehending S, as it is essentially in itself, requires adopting one particular point of view or perspective, namely that provided by undergoing S. The perspectival character of these states is, I believe, a reflection of the concepts that are deployed in thinking about or understanding these states from the inside. Without such an understanding, phenomenal states intuitively cannot be *fully* understood.

Consider again the case of pain. Fully understanding pain requires grasping how it feels, its distinctive phenomenal character, what it is like to undergo pain. That, in turn, requires applying to pain the concept that is typically applied when people introspect pain and pay attention to what it is like subjectively. This concept is a phenomenal concept. A person who lacks the phenomenal concept *pain* thereby is prevented from possessing the kind of understanding of pain provided by introspection. For such a person, there is a way of understanding pain that lies beyond his or her grasp. Consequently, such a person does not *fully* understand pain, as it is essentially in itself. And this is so whether or not the state of pain is itself physical.

My suggestion, then, is that the perspectival subjectivity of phenomenal states goes hand in hand with the perspectival character of phenomenal concepts, where phenomenal concepts are the concepts utilized when a person introspects his or her phenomenal state and forms a conception of what it is like for him or her at that time. Given the perspectival nature of indexical concepts, it may now be tempting to suppose that phenomenal concepts just are indexical concepts applied via introspection to phenomenal states.[4] This temptation is one that a physicalist (or functionalist) should resist, however, even though it is certainly true that we do often conceive of our phenomenal states in a manner that brings to bear indexical as well as phenomenal concepts.

For one thing, the perspective in the case of indexical concepts is very different from that which is relevant to phenomenal concepts. What is characteristic of indexical concepts is that they all involve an *egocentric* perspective. Each subject of psychological states, in thinking of something under an indexical concept, is thinking of it via a mode of presentation that bears an a priori connection to the first person concept *I*. For example, in thinking of the place I am in as here, I exercise the indexical concept *here* and this concept is such that I can know a priori that I am here.[5] Similarly, in thinking of something as *this* object, I exercise the concept *this* and this concept is such that I can know a priori that this thing is the object I am attending to (if I am attending to anything at all). Likewise, in thinking of the time as now, I exercise the concept *now* and this concept is such that I can know a priori that I am here now. Each indexical concept, then, is a priori linked with the concept *I* and thereby each indexical concept incorporates a certain perspective, namely the very special, first-person perspective each person has on himself. In the case of phenomenal concepts, however, the relevant perspective is not the generic first-person one. Grasping the phenomenal concept *pain*, for example, requires more than having a first-person perspective on oneself. As noted earlier, the relevant perspective or point of view is that conferred upon one by one's undergoing an experience of pain. Each phenomenal concept is thus tied to a *particular* experience-specific perspective occupied by the possessor of the concept. As the experiences vary, so too do the phenomenal concepts.

Another objection to identifying phenomenal concepts with indexical concepts is that if the phenomenal aspect of pain is physical (or functional), then an indexical conception of it can be formed from an external perspective by the person who is incapable of feeling pain. Such a person might think of the phenomenal character I experience on some given occasion when I feel pain as *that* quality. Clearly, this person would not have the same cognitive "fix" on the quality as I have on the inside. Intuitively, her demonstrative conception of it would be very different from my phenomenal one. Were this not so, she would not be able to make a significant *discovery* about the way pain feels if a neurological operation subsequently permitted her to experience pain. This does not show, of course, that *no* demonstrative is at play in the phenomenal conception. But it does indicate that some additional concept is being exercised that is not operative in the external conception—a general phenomenal concept.

What, then, is distinctive about our phenomenal concepts? What marks them out as special? I now turn to these questions.

2.2   Phenomenal Concepts

Phenomenal concepts, I have suggested, are not third-person concepts; neither are they just indexical concepts: they are conceptually irreducible. That is, no a priori analysis can be given of them in nonphenomenal terms. Phenomenal concepts, I have also suggested, are perspectival.

Consider, for example, the concept *pain* and suppose, for the sake of simplicity only, that this concept is purely phenomenal. The person who lacks the capacity to feel pain does not possess the phenomenal concept *pain* though she may acquire a nonphenomenal concept of pain. Intuitively, possessing the phenomenal concept requires knowing what it is like to experience pain. Likewise, in the case of the phenomenal concept *red*, a concept that is exercised when one becomes aware via introspection of what it is like to experience red.[6] Possession of the concept requires that one know what it is like to experience red.[7]

David Lewis (1990) has claimed that knowing what it is like to undergo an experience is a matter of having certain abilities, specifically, the abilities to remember the experience, to imagine it, to recognize it in a direct and immediate way when it comes again. As discussed in chapter 1, this view encounters certain difficulties. But intuitively, Lewis is surely right to draw *a* conceptual connection between knowing what it is like and the abilities specified above.[8] Given that phenomenal concept possession itself conceptually requires knowing what it is like, there thus emerges an a priori connection between phenomenal concept possession and the Lewis abilities. This connection finds direct support in the view that our concept of a phenomenal concept is that of a concept which plays a characteristic functional role—a role whose a priori specification entails that any possessor of the concept have the pertinent phenomenal abilities.

Phenomenal concepts, I maintain, are conceptually irreducible concepts that function in the right sort of way. To possess the phenomenal concept *red*, for example, is to possess a simple concept that has been acquired by undergoing experiences of red (barring neurosurgery to induce the state or a miracle) and that not only disposes one to form a visual image of red in response to a range of cognitive tasks pertaining to red but also is brought to bear in discriminating the experience of red from other color experiences in a direct and immediate manner via introspection. The functional role that the concept plays is what makes it perspectival. A person who is blind from birth or who is always restricted to an environment of things with achromatic colors cannot possess a concept with the requisite role and hence cannot possess the phenomenal concept *red*.[9] Let me now try to motivate this approach to phenomenal concepts further.

Consider first the following example of a phenomenal-physical identity claim:

The visual experience of red = brain state *B*.[10]

One reaction some philosophers have to claims of this sort is that they must be mistaken, since the phenomenology isn't captured by the right-hand side. From the present perspective, this reaction involves a sense/reference confusion. When we think of the referent of the designator on the left-hand side in a phenomenal way, we bring it under a concept that has a distinctive functional role. In reflecting on the identity claim and what is puzzling about it, the phenomenal concept we deploy is apt to trigger in us a visual image of red.[11] In this event, if the identity is true, our brain actually goes into brain state *B*. But, of course, when we think of the referent of the designator on the right-hand side *as* brain state *B*, nothing like that happens. Exercising the neurophysiological concept is not apt to trigger a visual image of red. It may then be tempting to infer that the right-hand side has left out the phenomenology of the left, that there is a huge gap the physicalist has failed to close. This conclusion clearly does not follow, however. There is indeed a striking difference in the roles that the concepts play, in their functioning, but not (so far as is shown here) in their referents.[12]

Second, it seems to us that we have a direct and immediate cognitive access to certain qualities when we introspect our experiences and feelings.[13] These qualities—phenomenal qualities, as we might call them—are ones that intuitively we know in a specially intimate way. The intuition that there is a direct and immediate access to such qualities (under normal conditions) needs to be preserved. The proposal I have made does that in a natural and straightforward manner. In being cognitively aware of our own phenomenal states, we subsume those states under phenomenal concepts. These concepts are simple. They are also, in part, *direct recognitional* concepts. For it is part of their characteristic functional role, *qua* phenomenal concepts, that they enable us to discriminate phenomenal qualities and states *directly* on the basis of introspection. In having the phenomenal concept *pain*, for example, I have a simple way of classifying pain that enables me to recognize it via introspection without the use of any associated reference-fixing intermediaries. Thus, it is guaranteed by the fact that the concept I am applying is phenomenal that I do not know introspectively that I am in pain *by* knowing something else connected to pain. My knowledge is direct and immediate. Introspection of the phenomenal character of pain causally triggers in me the application of the concept *pain* (under conditions of normal functioning of the introspective mechanism). Thereby, via the operation of a reliable process, I know that I am in pain.

Third, the thesis that phenomenal concepts are conceptually irreducible in the elucidated way explains why Mary, the brilliant color scientist who has always been locked in a black and white room (Jackson 1982), cannot *deduce* what it is like to experience the chromatic colors while she is imprisoned. No matter how hard she thinks about the exhaustive physical and functional information at her disposal, it won't suffice for her to possess the phenomenal color concepts of people with normal color vision. Lacking such concepts, Mary has no idea how such-and-such physical states visually feel. Thus, she certainly cannot deduce how they feel from the physical and functional facts.

Relatedly, the proposal I have made also explains why, intuitively, the phenomenal facts cannot be deduced a priori from the objective, physical, and functional facts, even by someone who possesses the requisite phenomenal concepts and who reflects upon them a priori in conjunction with the physical, and functional truths. Suppose, for example, that I am presented with all the objective, physical, and functional facts about what is going on in your brain and body at some time *t*. Suppose, moreover, that, within my repertoire of phenomenal concepts, I have the concepts necessary to conceptualize correctly what it is like for you at *t*. Intuitively, armchair reflection upon my phenomenal concepts and the physical and functional truths will not enable me to *deduce* how your state "feels" on the inside. Why should this be? After all, such a deduction *is* possible in the case of, say, the fact that there is water in some given place *p* on earth and the underlying physical facts.[14] Given my knowledge of an a priori truth of the form

(1) Water = the F (or an F),

where 'F' is an objective, physical, or functional predicate (e.g., "bearer of enough of the following features: being a liquid, filling lakes and oceans, coming out of taps, being called 'water' by English-speaking experts, being necessary for life on the planet, falling from the sky"), together with knowledge of the physical/functional truth

(2) H_2O = the F,

and the physical truth

(3) There is H_2O is in place p,

I may deduce

(4) There is water is in place p.[15]

Why is it that, intuitively, no corresponding deduction is possible in the phenomenal case?

The answer, I suggest, is that, where phenomenal concepts are concerned, there is no requisite a priori truth of the sort found in (1). This needs a little explanation. In the case of a natural kind concept such as the concept *water*, it seems plausible to suppose that the reference is fixed via a description. One who thinks of water thinks of it under some such description as "the liquid that comes out of taps, fills lakes, falls from the sky, and so forth." The description fixes the reference of the term 'water', but the complex property it expresses is only contingently associated with the kind (H_2O) 'water' rigidly designates. 'Water' designates, in each possible world (in which it designates anything), the natural kind that has a certain cluster of manifest features in our world. Here, then, there is indeed a suitable a priori truth about water for a deduction of the above sort, namely, "Water is the bearer of such-and-such manifest properties." This truth is contingent, but there is a corresponding necessary a priori truth that would have done as well, namely, "Water is the *actual* bearer of such-and-such manifest properties."

Appropriate a priori truths paralleling (1) are available for other third-person, objective concepts. Similar deductions can thus be constructed in these cases.[16] In the case of phenomenal concepts, however, matters are different. As noted above, one who has the phenomenal concept *pain*, for example, has a simple, recognitional concept. It functions in such a way that one can tell directly via introspection whether the distinctive phenomenal quality of pain is present without relying upon any additional clues. The phenomenal concept *pain* does not reach out to its referent via an associated description. More generally, no amount of a priori reflection on phenomenal concepts alone will reveal phenomenal-physical or phenomenal-functional connections, even of a contingent type.

This is evidenced by the widespread agreement that actual qualia inversions are *epistemically* possible. A priori reflection upon the phenomenal concept needed to conceptualize correctly what it is like for you at time *t* (call your phenomenal state '*S*' and the relevant phenomenal concept '*PC(S)*') does not rule out a priori the epistemic possibility that, in some other actual people, some phenomenal state other than *S* occupies the objective, functional role associated with *S* in you. Intuitively, cases of absent qualia are also epistemically possible. It could conceivably turn out that, in some actual people, *no* phenomenal state occupies the role *S* occupies in you. Likewise, intuitively, nothing in the character of phenomenal concepts guarantees a priori that there are no actual cases of physical duplicates with inverted or absent qualia. It surely is not a priori true, then, that *S* is the *F*, where '*F*' uses only objective, physical or functional vocabulary and '*S*' expresses a purely phenomenal concept for the phenomenal character of your state at *t*.

It does not help to propose, as one's candidate a priori truth for the deduction, the weaker "*S* is *an F*" (where '*S*' and '*F*' are interpreted as above). Once again, no suitable a priori truth (contingent or necessary) is available. In this case, although the a priori possibility of actual cases of absent and inverted qualia is no longer relevant (for even granting such cases, *S* is still *an* occupant of the *S* role, for example), other a priori possibilities may be brought to bear. Thus, it could conceivably turn out that phenomenal state *S* does not actually have any of its standard physical causes and effects (and so does not occupy the *S* role). Epiphenomenalism with respect to the physical, for example, is surely an a priori possibility for phenomenal state *S*, as is the thesis that some evil demon is the real cause of its occurrence in the actual world. It is even a priori consistent with our phenomenal concepts that we, in fact, have no physical bodies, that the phenomenal appearances are radically in error.

To illustrate further the point just made about about causes and effects: suppose that you are introspecting your current experience and in so doing you bring to bear *PC(S)*. Were you to find out that your experience actually has no physical effects—that some other state of you is the real cause of those physical goings-on you had previously taken *S* to produce—or were you to become convinced that some of your experiences, of which your present experience is one, actually have supernatural causes, you surely would not thereby have a license to infer that your experience does not "feel" to you on the inside as you judge from introspection, that *PC(S)* does not apply. This is not to say that if initially you take yourself to be feeling pain, say, you would automatically be in error to revise your view and to declare now that you are not feeling pain; my point concerns phenomenal concepts. And arguably, there is *a* concept of pain that is functional rather than phenomenal.

We are now ready to turn our attention to the alleged explanatory gap.

2.3   The Gap Examined

Consider the "gap" question "Why does physical state P feel like this?" Just how is this question to be understood? Evidently, it is not a question about the causation of phenomenal states since causation is a diachronic relation, and the question is posed with respect to a felt state (or quality) and a *simultaneously* occurring physical state. Nor is the question intended to presuppose that state P is the object of the feeling (the answer to the question "What is felt?"). What the question is really asking is why it is that to be in physical state P is thereby to have a feeling with this phenomenal character.

So interpreted, the question need not be taken as a question about identity. For even though the explanatory gap is one that supposedly confronts the physicalist and that, according to those who press the gap, prima facie indicates that something important is missing from the physicalist's account, the question still arises even if it is denied that this feeling is one and the same as P. Consider, by way of comparison, the question "Why is it that to have no hairs on one's head is thereby to be bald?" This question is not asking why having no head hairs is one and the same as being bald; evidently one can be bald without having zero hairs on one's head. The question is best taken to ask why having no hairs *suffices* for being bald; and the answer, of course, is that being bald is one and the same as having sufficiently few head hairs and having no head hairs is a *realization* of having sufficiently few.

Understood in a parallel way, the physicalist can respond that the explanatory gap question has a straightforward answer: this feeling is one and the same as a certain higher-level physical state Q, and P realizes Q (just as in the earlier case of digestion, the action of enzymes in the alimentary canal realizes the process of digestion). To be in P, then, is thereby to have a feeling with this phenomenal character rather than to have a feeling with some other phenomenal character or to be in a state that is not a feeling at all, since being in a state with this phenomenal character = being in Q, and P realizes Q rather than a physical state with which some other feeling (or no feeling) is identical.

No doubt it will be said that this reply by the physicalist merely shifts the focus of the puzzle from P to whatever higher-level physical state Q is chosen. Why is Q identical with this feeling? Why shouldn't Q be another feeling or no feeling?

One interpretation of the question about identity is purely referential. Take the referent of the term 'Q' and the referent of the term 'this feeling'—conceive of those referents as you will—why is the former the same as the latter? If this is how the question is understood, then there is no significant question here for the physicalist. Only one state exists, conceived of in two ways, and that state must be self-identical. On this interpretation, then, there is no need for an answer and no explanatory gap.

On an alternative concept-dependent reading, the question may be understood to ask why the physical concept expressed by 'Q' picks out the same state as the appropriate phenomenal concept (whichever concept is utilized in introspecting this feeling and forming a conception of its phenomenal character). One natural way to take the force of the term 'why' here is as a request for cogent empirical reasons to believe that the concepts have the same referent. Taken this way, asking the question "Why is Q this feeling?" is like asking why Jones is the candidate most likely to be elected. In the latter case, evidently what is wanted are empirical reasons in support of the de dicto belief that Jones is the candidate most likely to be elected, for example, that Jones has the backing of Smith, that Smith can raise more money for Jones than can be raised for any other candidate, and that campaign money is the most important factor in getting elected.[17] Here, then, the given hypothesis is deduced from (or perhaps inductively corroborated by) a posteriori claims which express the empirical evidence for the hypothesis.

Understood in this way, the question "Why is physical state Q this feeling?" has an answer of the following general sort: this feeling is physical (for how else are we to account for its causal efficacy with respect to behavior, given the very plausible empirical hypothesis that there are no nonphysical causes of the physical?) and among the physical states, Q is the best candidate for identification with this feeling, all things considered (i.e., Q does the best job at explaining the range of facts concerning phenomenal consciousness we want explained[18]). So here there is a justification of the hypothesis that physical state Q = this feeling from empirical premises, and there is no explanatory gap between the presence of Q and the presence of that particular type of feeling.

Suppose it is now denied that what is wanted is a straightforward wholly empirical justification of the sort just provided. Suppose it is said that it is not enough to appeal to the physical facts and some appropriate a posteriori premises about experiences or feelings. What is wanted, rather, is an a priori demonstration or deduction of the given identity from physical facts about Q *and no further information of an empirical sort*. With such a demonstration, we will have an answer to the question along the following lines: Q = this feeling (e.g., the feeling of pain) since (a) it is an empirical, physical truth that Q = the F, where 'F' is physical, and (b) it is also a priori true that this feeling (e.g., the feeling of pain) = the F[19]. Understood in this way, however, as shown in section 2.2, the character of phenomenal concepts and the way they differ from third-person concepts conceptually guarantees that the question has no answer.[20] But if it is a conceptual truth that the question can't be answered, then there can't be an explanation of the relevant sort, *whatever* the future brings. Since an explanatory *gap* exists only if there is something unexplained that needs explaining, and something needs explaining only if it can be explained (whether or not it lies within the power of *human beings* to explain it), there is again no gap.

Whichever interpretation is adopted, then, the explanatory gap is unreal. In supposing otherwise, in insisting that there must be an answer to the question, "Why does so-and-so physical state feel such-and-such way?" that lies beyond our current grasp—an answer as complete and satisfying as our answers to the counterpart questions for solidity and digestion—we find ourselves the victims of a cognitive illusion induced by a failure to recognize the special character of phenomenal concepts. There is no such answer; neither is there any threat to physicalism or functionalism. What needs explaining is only why philosophers have been under the *illusion* that there is a troublesome explanatory gap. That explanation I have provided.

2.4 Remaining Worries

Suppose that the question, "Why is Q identical with this feeling?" is viewed as requesting cogent, empirical reasons in support of the hypothesis that Q is this feeling. Then, it may be argued, contrary to what I supposed earlier, the question *cannot* be answered by saying that this feeling is physical (given its causal efficacy) and, among the physical states, Q is the best candidate for identification with it, all things considered. The reason is that, given what we currently know about phenomenal consciousness, to settle on Q rather than some other physical state would be quite arbitrary. As things now stand, we have no nonarbitrary way of selecting the privileged physical state. Here, it may be said, lies the real explanatory gap for consciousness.

My reply begins with the observation that there is a clear range of commonsense facts that any theory of phenomenal consciousness needs to explain—for example: the fact that I cannot experience your pains, itches, tickles, and so on; the fact that pains, itches, tickles cannot exist unowned; the fact that phenomenal character is causally efficacious with respect to behavior; the fact that experience is transparent[21]; the fact that something can look F, in the phenomenal sense of the term 'look', without looking G, even if 'F' and 'G' are coextensive;[22] the fact that people can feel sensations in phantom limbs; the fact that I can feel a pain in a finger when my finger is in my mouth without thereby feeling a pain in my mouth; the fact that an afterimage can be green, say, without anything in the brain being green.

This list is only partial, of course, even with respect to the commonsense facts, and I certainly do not mean to deny that further relevant facts may be discovered in the future. My point is that the known facts are sufficiently varied and rich that we are justified in accepting whatever philosophical theory of the phenomenal best explains them. Such a theory, I maintain, will inevitably restrict itself to the physical, given that there are no nonphysical causes. And that there is a suitable theory that wins out over others, all things considered, seems to me clear.[23] In my view, then, the claim that we have no way of nonarbitrarily selecting the privileged physical state is without foundation.

Another very different worry that may be raised with respect to the position I have taken focuses upon phenomenal concepts. If the special features of phenomenal concepts are largely responsible for the supposition that a perplexing explanatory gap exists between phenomenal "feels" and the underlying physical goings-on, then, it may be suggested, a new gap now arises at the level of concepts. For, letting the phenomenal concept of pain be $PC(\text{pain})$, the proposed view naturally leads us to ask, "Why does the application of $PC(\text{pain})$ to physical state P ensure that P feels like *this*?" This gap, it may be urged, is just as challenging as the original one. Thus, the problem hasn't really been solved; rather, it has been kicked upstairs, from the level of reference to that of sense.

What is needed to answer this worry is a full appreciation of the relationship between phenomenal concepts and phenomenal 'feels'. Phenomenal concepts are exercised (in the first person case) in our *awareness* of our phenomenal states via introspection. They enable us to become aware of the felt character of our phenomenal states. Without such concepts, we would be 'blind' to our 'feels'. We would be in much the same state as the distracted driver of chapter 1 who is thinking hard about philosophy, say, as he drives along the highway. The driver is unaware of how the road ahead looks to him, of the visual experiences he is undergoing. But the experiences are still there. He still *sees* the road ahead.

Now the explanatory gap for consciousness is supposedly a gap between the 'feels' and the underlying physical/functional states. It arises, however, only for creatures sophisticated enough to be able to introspect their phenomenal states and reflect upon them. So, the explanatory gap would not arise for a creature that lacked any phenomenal concepts. Once the concepts are in the creature's repertoire, the creature can raise and be perplexed by the explanatory gap question. The awareness of the gap, the appreciation of the supposed problem, demands phenomenal concepts; but the gap itself concerns the 'feels', not the concepts.

Cognitive awareness of our own feelings itself feels no special way at all. Phenomenal character attaches to experiences and feelings (including images), and not, I maintain, to our cognitive responses to them.[24] Admittedly, as I noted earlier, phenomenal concepts are concepts that dispose their possessors to form images or phenomenal memories of the relevant experiences (among other things); but the concepts themselves do not have an experiential character.

In my view, then, the question "Why does the application of PC(pain) to physical state P ensure that P feels like *this*?" is based upon a mistaken presupposition. The application of PC(pain) does not ensure that P feels any way. Nor does it ensure that the awareness of P feels like *this*. For the *awareness* of P does not feel any way. So, there really isn't a genuine counterpart question for phenomenal concepts. And without such a question, there certainly isn't a higher level explanatory gap.

The final worry I want to address is one that arises out of my supposition that there is an important disanalogy between the case of natural kind concepts and that of phenomenal concepts. Natural kind concepts are rigid: each such concept picks out the same kind in every possible world in which it picks out anything. But, as noted earlier, reference is fixed to a given kind in the actual world (at least in part) via an associated description citing characteristic effects or manifest features of the kind. The concept *heat*, for example, gets its reference fixed to the natural kind it rigidly denotes, namely, molecular motion, via some such associated description as "the cause of certain characteristic bodily reactions (e.g., temperature increase, sweating, dehydration)." The property attributed by this reference-fixing description ('the R' for short), of course, is not a priori associated with the theoretical concept *molecular motion*. We discover by empirical investigation that molecular motion is the R, and thereby, given the a priori truth that heat is the R, we establish by a posteriori means that heat is molecular motion. Since the kind concept *molecular motion*, like other such concepts, is rigid, the identity between heat and molecular motion is both necessary and a posteriori.

In the case of phenomenal concepts, however, I have denied that there are any descriptive reference fixers. Phenomenal concepts, in my view, are rigid designators, but they do not refer to phenomenal qualities (or the states whose essences are such qualities) via *other* qualities that users of the concepts a priori associate with them. One who thinks of the phenomenal state of pain under the phenomenal concept *pain* thinks of pain directly as pain. I have also claimed that there is no gap in the world between the phenomenal and the objective, physical (or functional) goings-on. I am thus committed to the thesis that certain phenomenal-physical (or functional) identity claims are necessary, a posteriori truths. Some (e.g., Braddon-Mitchell and Jackson 1996, Chalmers 1996) will say that this is an unhappy, indeed unstable, combination of views.

This criticism gets its force from the supposition (*S*) that a sentence of the type "$D_1 = D_2$" expresses a necessary truth that is also a posteriori only if one or other of the rigid concepts expressed by 'D_1' and 'D_2' picks out its referent via an associated property distinct from that referent to which the other concept cannot be linked just by a priori reflection. It should be noted, however, that this supposition does not require that the relevant concept always be a nontheoretical one. Indeed, we know that this cannot be the case, given the existence of wholly theoretical or scientific identity statements. Consider, for example,

Hydrogen = so-and-so quantum-mechanical system,

where "so-and-so quantum mechanical system" is fleshed out so as to form a suitable rigid description. That claim, if true, is necessarily true. But it is evidently a posteriori. So, according to (*S*), one or more of the two theoretical concepts expressed by the designators flanking the identity sign must pick out its referent via a distinct property to which the other bears only an a posteriori connection. And that condition is met. For it is surely no less reasonable to suppose that the concept *hydrogen* refers via a description, for example, "whatever passes the chemical tests for the stuff called 'hydrogen'" (or something to that effect) than it is to suppose that the concept *water* has its referent fixed via a description. The complex property expressed by the description of hydrogen is not a priori linked to the relevant complex quantum-mechanical concept.

This point can be put to use by the advocate of phenomenal/physical (or functional) identities. Consider, for example, the identity claim "Pain

= B," where 'B' is a rigid designator for a brain state.[25] The concept B, like the concept *hydrogen*, can plausibly be held to have an a priori associated reference-fixing description citing appropriate laboratory tests, or perhaps the appearance of brain state B under a cerebroscope. Since the connection between the property expressed by this description and the phenomenal concept *pain* is evidently a posteriori, there is no difficulty in holding that "Pain = B" is a necessary a posteriori truth.

Suppose, however, that the identity claim uses a rigid description on the right-hand side, for example, "the firing of C-fibers," to take an old philosophical favorite, instead of a rigid name. Once again there is no problem. Since the phenomenal concept *pain* is not a priori connected to the property attributed by the description, the identity between pain and the firing of C-fibers will be a posteriori.

To summarize: phenomenal concepts are very special concepts, in some ways like indexical concepts. But they are not one and the same as indexical concepts. A failure to appreciate the special and a priori irreducible character of phenomenal concepts misleads us into thinking that there is a deep and puzzling explanatory gap for phenomenal consciousness. But this is an illusion. There is no such gap. Those who see in the alleged gap a reason for supposing that phenomenal qualities are special qualities, different in kind from anything physical or functional are *doubly* mistaken. Consciousness is indeed a wonderful thing, as Woody Allen said, but it is not so wonderful that it is magical. Why, it is, I suppose, even found in New Jersey!

Notes

1. The expression "explanatory gap" was coined by Joseph Levine (1983). The first philosopher to have used the term 'gap' in connection with consciousness (to my knowledge) was Du Bois-Reymond (1885–87).

2. This view seems to trace back to Du Bois-Reymond 1885–87.

3. In some places in this chapter, I distinguish 'functional' from 'physical'. Elsewhere, however, for ease of exposition, I use the term 'physical' more broadly so that a functional type with a physical realization counts as physical, as does a similarly realized representational type. Nothing of substance hangs upon this usage.

4. I take an indexical concept to be one that changes its reference from context of exercise to context of exercise. So understood, the demonstrative concept *this* is indexical.

5. What if I am a disembodied spirit? Arguably I am still here (in this place) even though my body is merely apparent. An alternative view is that what is a priori is that I am here, if I am in any place at all.

6. On my view, one becomes aware of what it is like to experience red by becoming aware (via introspection) that one is experiencing red. Those who take the position that there can be phenomenally inverted color experiences, each of which is nonetheless properly classified as the experience of red, will want to deny that there is such a single phenomenal concept as *red*. Instead, there will be any number of general concepts, each of which refers to a different phenomenal quality (whichever quality in the user of the concept is associated with experiencing red). This difference makes no difference for present purposes. The points I make below with respect to the phenomenal concept *red* can be restated with respect to the appropriate preferred person-specific concepts. I use the example of *red* here in part because of my own theory about the nature of phenomenal character (see Tye, 1995, and chapter 3 in this volume) and in part for simplicity.

7. Let me stress that this is true only for the *phenomenal* concept *red*. It is not true of the nonphenomenal concept of red, a concept normally sighted people share with blind people, for example.

8. This connection, in my view, is as follows: one knows what it is like to experience *P* only if he/she has the Lewis *P*-involving abilities, if *P* is no longer present.

9. Cf. Harman (1990) and Tye (1995).

10. Of course, I myself do not accept identities of this sort. In my view, the objective states with which phenomenal states should be identified are complex representational states. For present purposes, however, this not matter.

11. I do not mean to suggest here that the exercise of a phenomenal concept is always apt to trigger an image. In the case of the phenomenal concept *pain*, for example, a phenomenal response may well be triggered in the form of a phenomenal memory of the feeling of pain (with the result that one shudders or grimaces a bit in reflecting upon the relevant identity claim). But this memory need not take the form of an image (unless the term 'image' is understood very broadly indeed).

12. Cf. Papineau 1994.

13. In my view, the qualities of which we are directly aware when we introspect our experiences are not qualities *of* the experiences but rather qualities the experiences represent. This issue is not relevant here but is pursued in chapter 3.

14. Not everyone accepts this claim. See note 15.

15. See Braddon-Mitchell and Jackson (1996, p. 133). Some dispute that such a deduction is possible even in the water/H_2O case. See, for example, Block and

Stalnaker, 1999b. Their argument seems to me unpersuasive. Block and Stalnaker mistakenly suppose that if (2) is to count as an appropriate truth for use in the deduction, it must be a priori entailed by the microphysical truths alone, and they then challenge that claim by noting that it is a priori consistent with the microphysical facts that in the actual world there is a *nonphysical* entity, ghost water, as well as H_2O (so that while H_2O is an F, it is not the F). However, the obvious reply is that what is required for (2)'s inclusion in the premises is that (2) be a physical truth, where a physical truth is not one that is a priori entailed by the microphysical truths simpliciter but, rather, a truth that is a priori entailed by the conjunction of the microphysical truths and the claim that the actual world is a minimal (micro)physical duplicate of itself. In the a priori scenario Block and Stanaker describe, the actual world is *not* a minimal (micro)physical duplicate of itself. So, that scenario is simply irrelevant. I owe this point to Brian McLaughlin. For a definition of the term 'minimal physical duplicate', see Braddon-Mitchell and Jackson, ibid., chapter 1. It is also worth noting that in (1) the definite description 'the F' is not required—an indefinite description will suffice.

16. These deductions will not always use an identity claim at step (2). For example, where Q and R are states, the deduction will often take the following general form: Q = the state of having a state that occupies the F role; R (in Xs) occupies the F role; there is an X in state R at place p; therefore, there is an X in state Q at place p.

17. This example involves a descriptive concept. But the use of a descriptive concept is not essential to my point. If a similar question were raised in terms of Hesperus and Phosperus, the absence of a descriptive analysis of the names would not jeopardize an answer that cited straightforwardly astronomical reasons.

18. For more on this topic, see this chapter, p. 35.

19. The term 'feeling' in 'this feeling' itself expresses a phenomenal concept, as (I am supposing) does the term 'pain' here.

20. This claim is also made by Scott Sturgeon in his 1994. In this essay, Sturgeon constructs a taxonomy of explanatory strategies and argues that none of them is applicable to solving what he calls "the problem of qualia." His explanation of their inapplicability appeals to the special epistemic features of qualia concepts. Sturgeon's conclusion is that "it is conceptually impossible to explain subjective experience in nonsubjective terms" (p. 235). That blanket claim seems to me too strong, given the different ways of interpreting the 'gap' question. But, on the current interpretation, I agree with Sturgeon.

21. Some philosophers (e.g., Block, 1990) deny that this is a fact. But properly explicated (see chapter 3), it seems to me an undeniable datum that any philosophical theory worth its salt needs to preserve.

22. For more on this subject, see chapter 3.

23. The theory is representationalism. See Tye (1995) and chapters 3–6 in this volume. Once again, I use the term 'physical' broadly (see note 3).

24. I do not deny that some cognitive responses have associated linguistic, auditory images. In saying that phenomenal character attaches to experiences and feelings, I do not mean to commit myself to the view that phenomenal character is a quality of experiences and feelings. Indeed, I reject that view (see chapter 3).

25. Again, this is not my own view. I use this identity for illustrative purposes only.

II

Representationalism

3

Representationalism: The Theory and Its Motivations

Representationalism is a thesis about the phenomenal character of experiences, about their immediate subjective 'feel'.[1] At a minimum, the thesis is one of supervenience: necessarily, experiences that are alike in their representational contents are alike in their phenomenal character. So understood, the thesis is silent on the nature of phenomenal character. Strong or pure representationalism goes further. It aims to tell us what phenomenal character *is*. According to the theory developed in Tye 1995, phenomenal character is one and the same as representational content that meets certain further conditions. This view has two primary motivations, both of which deserve further discussion. I begin with the appeal to the so-called "transparency of experience."

3.1 Transparency

I believe that experience is transparent. I also believe that its transparency is a very powerful motivation for the representationalist view. I concede, however, that the appeal to transparency has not been well understood. I will therefore try to clarify the appeal by presenting it, or at least my version of it, step by step, in full detail.

Step 1

Focus your attention on the scene before your eyes and on how things *look* to you. You see various objects; and you see these objects by seeing their facing surfaces. Sense-datum theorists claimed that the facing surfaces of the objects are themselves seen by seeing further immaterial surfaces or sense data. The sense-datum theory is unacceptable, however, for a whole host of familiar reasons. Intuitively, the surfaces you see directly are publicly observable physical surfaces.[2] They are at varying angles to the line of sight and varying distances away. They can be photographed. In seeing these surfaces, you are immediately and directly aware of a whole host of qualities. You may not be able to name or describe these qualities but they look to you to qualify the surfaces;[3] you experience them as being qualities of the surfaces. None of the qualities of which you are directly aware in seeing the various surfaces look to you to be qualities of your experience. You do not experience any of these qualities as qualities of your experience. For example, if blueness is one of the qualities and round-ness another, you do not experience your experience as blue or round. Note the use of the word 'if' here. At this stage, no definite claim is being made as to the identity of the relevant qualities. Sydney Shoemaker, for example, denies that we are directly aware of colors in visual experience whereas I hold that we are. Indeed, Shoemaker (1990) maintains that the qualities of which we are directly aware are relational qualities of exter-nal surfaces that involve relations to intrinsic qualities of experiences (although we are not aware of them as such). So long as the latter quali-ties—the ones possessed by the experiences—are not qualities of which we are directly aware when we introspect our experiences (and Shoemaker accepts that they are not), this disagreement between Shoemaker and myself does not threaten step 1.[4]

Step 2
To suppose that the qualities of which perceivers are directly aware in undergoing ordinary, everyday visual experiences are really qualities of the experiences would be to convict such experiences of massive error. That is just not credible. It seems totally implausible to hold that visual experience is systematically misleading in this way. Accordingly, the qualities of which you are directly aware in focusing on the scene before your eyes and how things look are not qualities of your visual experience.

Step 3
If you are attending to how things *look* to you, as opposed to how they are independent of how they look, you are bringing to bear your faculty of introspection. But in so doing, you are not aware of any inner object

or thing. The only objects of which you are aware are the external ones making up the scene before your eyes. Nor, to repeat, are you directly aware of any qualities of your experience. Your experience is thus transparent to you. But when you introspect, you are certainly aware of the phenomenal character of your visual experience. On the basis of introspection, you know what it is like for you visually on the given occasion. Via introspection, you are directly aware of a range of qualities that you experience as being qualities of surfaces at varying distances away and orientations *and thereby* you are aware of the phenomenal character of your experience. By being aware of the external qualities, you are aware of what it is like for you. This is not to say, of course, that you *infer* the phenomenal character of your experience from your awareness of the external qualities. Obviously no *reasoning* is involved. Still, by attending to what you experience outside, as it were, you know what it is like inside. Therefore, your awareness of phenomenal character is not the direct awareness of a quality of your experience. Relatedly, the phenomenal character itself is not a quality of your experience to which you have direct access.

This conclusion is one that the sense-datum theorists would have endorsed. Sense-datum theorists were at pains to distinguish the act of sensing from the thing sensed and they insisted that the qualities of which we are directly and immediately aware are qualities of the latter, specifically, an immaterial surface or sense datum (as noted in Step 1).[5] Thus, it should come as no surprise to find G. E. Moore, one of the chief advocates of the sense-datum theory, drawing our attention to the phenomenon of transparency in the following passages:

When we try to introspect the sensation of blue, all we can see is the blue: the other element is as if it were diaphonous. (1903, p. 25)

I do now see certain blackish marks on a whitish ground, and I hear certain sounds which I attribute to the ticking of my clock. . . . It seems to me quite evident that the relation to the marks which I express by saying that I *see* them is not different from the relation to the sounds which I express by saying that I *hear* them. . . . (1913, p. 173)

Step 4

The points made thus far do not require that your visual experience be veridical. Indeed, the case could be one of complete hallucination. The

objects and their surfaces could be unreal. Still, the phenomenal character of your visual experience is not a quality or cluster of qualities of
your experience to which you have direct access.

Step 5

As you view the scene before your eyes and how things look to you, necessarily, if any of the qualities of which you are *directly* aware change,
then the phenomenal character of your experience changes. Consider,
for example, the facing surface of a ripe tomato in a bowl before you. In
attending to the color of the tomato, you are directly aware of a certain
quality, Q, as covering that surface. You experience each just noticeable
part of the surface as having Q. Again, whether Q is itself a color or some
other quality, awareness of which mediates your awareness of color, is left
open here. But change Q—for example, by changing the color of the
tomato or by donning color-inverting lenses—and what it is like for you
in viewing the tomato necessarily changes. Facts like this one are surely
not brute. Moreover, they obtain even in the case that you are halluci-
nating. If the tomato does not exist, still you are directly aware of Q;
and if some other quality replaces Q, the phenomenal character of your
experience changes. An explanation is needed of why the phenomenal
character of visual experiences is sensitive in this way to surface qualities—qualities that, if they are qualities of anything at all, are qualities of
surfaces experienced. Given the conclusion of step 4, the explanation
surely is that the phenomenal character *involves* the surface qualities of
which the subject of the visual experience is directly aware—that these
qualities at least partly *constitute* phenomenal character.

Step 6

What, then, is visual phenomenal character? One possible hypothesis is
that it is a quality of the surface experienced. That hypothesis is intelli-
gible only if it is assumed that the surface is an immaterial one of the
sort the sense-datum theorists posited. The best hypothesis, I suggest, is
that visual phenomenal character is representational content of a certain
sort—content into which certain external qualities enter. This explains
why visual phenomenal character is not a quality of an experience to
which we have direct access (representational content is not a quality of

the thing that has representational content) and why visual phenomenal character necessarily changes with a change in the qualities of which one is directly aware (changing the qualities changes the content). It also explains why the phenomenal character of a visual experience is something the experience *has*—something that can be common to different token experiences—and why visual experiences have phenomenal character even if nothing really has the qualities of which one is directly aware via introspection.

Step 7

Visual phenomenal qualities or visual qualia are supposedly qualities of which the subjects of visual experiences are directly aware via introspection. Tradition has it that these qualities are qualities of the experiences. Tradition is wrong. There are no such qualities *of experiences*. If we stipulate that something is a visual phenomenal quality or a quale only if it is a directly accessible quality of an experience, then there are no visual phenomenal qualities or qualia. Still there are qualities of which the subjects of visual experiences are directly aware via introspection. They are qualities of external surfaces (and volumes and films[6]), if they are qualities of anything. These qualities, by entering into the appropriate representational contents of visual experiences, contribute to the phenomenal character of the experiences. Thus, they may reasonably be called "phenomenal qualities" in a less restrictive sense of the term.

Step 8

All of the above points generalize to other perceptual modalities. For example, we hear things by hearing the sounds they emit. These sounds are publicly accessible. They can be recorded. Similarly, we smell things by smelling the odors they give off. They, too, are publicly accessible. You and I can both smell the foul odor of the rotting garbage. Odors, like sounds, move through physical space. We taste things by tasting their tastes. One and the same taste can be tasted by different people. Some tastes are bitter, others are sweet. When we introspect our experiences of hearing, smelling, and tasting, the qualities of which we are directly aware are qualities we experience as being qualities of sounds, odors, and tastes. It seems very natural to suppose that among these qualities are the following: pitch, tone, loudness, pungency, muskiness, sweetness, salti-ness, sourness. But this supposition is not needed by the argument. The crucial point again is that the qualities of which we are directly aware via introspection—*whatever* they turn out to be—are not qualities of the experiences of hearing, smelling, and tasting. Rather, they are qualities of public surfaces, sounds, odors, tastes, and so forth, if they are qualities of anything at all (for, as before, the experiences may be hallucinatory). Change *these* qualities—the ones of which we can be directly aware via introspection—and, necessarily, the phenomenal character of the experi-ence changes. Again, then, phenomenal character is best taken to be a matter of representational content. And again, there are no phenomenal qualities, conceived of as qualities of experiences.

Step 9
The case of bodily sensations is treated in the same way. Let me give one illustration—that of experiencing pain in a finger. You can have a pain without noticing it, as, for example, when you are distracted for a moment by something else; but if you do notice a pain—if you are intro-spectively aware of it—then your attention goes to *wherever you feel the pain* (in this case, to your finger). Your attention does not go to where your experience is (that is, to your head, if your experience is a physical thing) or to nowhere at all. In attending to your pain, you are directly and immediately aware of a certain quality or cluster of qualities, which you experience as being in your finger. That quality or cluster of quali-ties is what you want so strongly to stop experiencing. As before, no claim is made as to the identity of this quality or cluster. Moreover, even if you are feeling a pain in a phantom finger, you are directly aware of a quality you strongly dislike, a quality that you *experience* as being in a finger, even though the finger no longer exists. The point to stress, then, is that the qualities of which we are all directly aware in introspecting pain experiences are not qualities of the experiences (assuming that no massive error occurs), but qualities of bodily disturbances in regions where the pains are felt to be, if they are qualities of anything. The argu-ment proceeds from here as in the cases of the experiences of seeing, hearing, smelling, and tasting.

Step 10

The previous steps may be generalized to the case of the phenomenal character of felt emotions and moods. In the case of emotions, the qualities of which one is directly aware in introspecting felt emotions are frequently localized in particular parts of the body and experienced as such. For example, if one feels sudden jealousy, one is likely to feel one's stomach sink, one's heart beat faster, one's blood pressure increase. Likewise, in the case of the feeling of fear or anger (Tye, 1995). With moods, however, the relevant qualities are usually not experienced as localized in this way. If one feels elated, one experiences a change in oneself *overall*. The qualities of which one is directly aware in attending to how one feels on such an occasion are experienced as qualities of *oneself*. One is aware of a general sense of buoyancy, of quickened reactions, of somehow being more alive. These qualities are not qualities of *one's experience*. One's feeling of elation is not buoyant or faster reacting or somehow more alive. Accordingly, transparency obtains here just as in the other cases. The explanation, moreover, is the same.

That, then, is how, in my view, the appeal to transparency should go.[7] Next I want to make a few remarks about the nature of introspective awareness of phenomenal character in light of the position adopted in this section.

3.2 Introspective Awareness of Phenomenal Character

When we introspect our experiences and feelings, we become aware of what it is like for us to undergo them. But we are not directly aware of those experiences and feelings; nor are we directly aware of any of their qualities. The qualities to which we have direct access are the external ones, the qualities that, if they are qualities of anything, are qualities of external things.[8] By being aware of these qualities, we are aware of phenomenal character. How can this be?

Patently, awareness of phenomenal character is not a quasi-scanning process. Our attention goes *outside* in the visual case, for example, not to the experience *inside* our heads. We attend to one thing—the external surfaces and qualities—and yet *thereby* we are aware of something else, the 'feel' of our experience. Awareness of that 'feel' is not direct awareness *of* a quality of the experience. It is awareness that is based upon direct awareness of external qualities without any inference or reasoning being involved. Introspective awareness of phenomenal character, I maintain, is awareness-*that*—awareness that *an* experience with a certain phenomenal character is present.

Consider the following situation, which is, in some important respects, parallel. I set a bomb to go off at 5 PM. At 5 PM, I am somewhere else, but I am looking at my watch. Seeing it read 5:00, I am aware that the bomb is now exploding, but I do not see the bomb. I am not directly aware *of* it. Nor am I directly aware *of* the bomb's qualities at 5 PM. For example, I am not directly aware of the quality of exploding. My awareness of the bomb is propositional. I judge that the bomb is exploding, and I do so by looking at my watch. By being aware of my watch and its qualities, I am aware that an event involving an object of which I am not directly aware is taking place elsewhere.

The case just presented is one of displaced perception or 'secondary' seeing-that (seeing that *P* by seeing something not involved in the truth conditions for the proposition that *P*). Introspection of phenomenal character is usefully modeled upon such cases.[9] But there are also some significant differences. My belief that the bomb is now exploding is based upon a background belief that when the watch reads 5:00, the bomb explodes, together with my awareness that the watch reads 5:00. Someone who lacked that background belief would not believe that the bomb is now exploding by looking at my watch at 5 PM. The background belief and the content of the perceptual awareness explain why the other belief state is present. They provide a propositional justification for that state. In the case of introspection of phenomenal character however, there is no corresponding justification. If I am aware of certain external qualities, I do not need a background belief to be aware that I am undergoing an experience with a certain phenomenal character once I introspect. The process is automatic. Introspection of phenomenal character is a *reliable* process that takes awareness *of* external qualities (in the case of perceptual sensations) as input and yields awareness *that* a state is present with a certain phenomenal character as output. It is the reliability of this process that underwrites knowledge of phenomenal character.

In this respect, introspection of phenomenal character is like introspection of thought contents. Let me explain.

If I think that water is wet and I introspect—I become aware *that* I am thinking that water is wet. This awareness is not based upon an inference from other propositional states. Nor is it the result of attention to an internal auditory image of myself saying that water is wet, though such an image may accompany my thought. Intuitively, my introspective access to what I am thinking is direct. It seems plausible to suppose that introspection of thought contents is a reliable process that takes as input the content of the thought and delivers as output a belief or judgment that one is undergoing a state with that content.

On this view of introspective knowledge of thought contents, the concept of a thought that *P* is, in its first-person present-tense application, a *recognitional* concept.[10] Those who have mastered the concept can introspectively recognize that an occurrent thought that *P* is present without going through any process of reasoning. In cases involving what Tyler Burge has called "Cogito thoughts" (that is, cases in which one consciously thinks to oneself that one is thinking that *P*), there is a conscious act of recognition. But it is often the case that one's recognition of what one is occurrently thinking does not involve a conscious act. One can recognize that one is thinking that water is a liquid when the only occurrent thought one is having is that water is a liquid.

In much the same way, we do not have introspective knowledge of phenomenal character by inferring that character from something else. We acquire introspective knowledge of what it is like to have such-and-such an experience or feeling via a reliable process that triggers the application of a suitable phenomenal concept or concepts. This reliable process, as noted earlier, takes as input the direct awareness of external qualities (in the perceptual case). Phenomenal concepts—the concepts that enable us to form a conception of phenomenal character via introspection—are, in my view, recognitional concepts of a special sort (described in chapter 2).

Phenomenal concepts do not inform their possessors that phenomenal character *is* a certain sort of content. The identification of the former with the latter is a hypothesis that is justified in terms of its explanatory power. Nothing in the character of phenomenal concepts rules out the possibility that the qualities of which we are directly aware, when we introspect, are really qualities of immaterial surfaces, or sensa, presented to us by material objects. Admittedly, these surfaces must be three-dimensional, in some sense, for they are experienced as such, and that patently requires further explanation. But the sense-datum possibility, in my view, is ultimately eliminated on additional grounds: its unnecessary complexity, its postulation of nonphysical causes (given that phenomenal character is causally efficacious), and its counterintuitiveness in denying that the surfaces of which we are directly aware are not just plain, old material surfaces. What introspection and phenomenal concepts rule out is the possibility that the qualities to which we have direct introspective access are qualities of experiences.

3.3   The Intensionality of Phenomenal Discourse

The second primary motivation for the representational approach to phenomenal character is the intensionality of phenomenal talk. Consider first 'looks' talk. Not all 'looks' talk is phenomenal. Roderick Chisholm (1957) and, following Chisholm, Frank Jackson (1977) suggest that locutions of the form "X looks F to S" and "X appears F to S," where 'F' expresses a sensory property (that is, a property of which one is directly aware via introspection as one undergoes a sensory experience) are phenomenal. These locutions, according to Chisholm and Jackson, are not equivalent to such locutions as "X looks as if it is F to S" (the epistemic use of 'looks') or "X looks like an F to S" (the comparative use). Something cannot look as if it is F to S unless S has the concept F; but, intuitively, something can look F to S without S's having the concept (see chapter 1, p. 11 and below, pp. 55–57). Moreover, something F can look like a G thing to S without looking G to S. For example, in a possible world in which light bends in funny ways and round things look elliptical while elliptical things look round, something round looks elliptical but it doesn't look like an ellipse (that is, it doesn't look the way ellipses look).

I agree with Chisholm and Jackson here and I take "X looks F to S," given an appropriate 'F,' to be a paradigm of phenomenal talk. This locution is intensional in two ways. First, it can be true that X looks F to S, even if there is no X. Second, it can be true that X looks F to S without X's looking G to S, even if 'F' and 'G' are coextensive. Suppose, for example, that I bang my head and I see stars.[11] Although there are no stars, it can still be true that the stars look bright to me. Alternatively suppose that, as it happens, everything purple is poisonous and everything poisonous is purple. Still, something, in looking purple to me, does not look poisonous. I may see it *as* poisonous; it may look to me *to be* poisonous. But it does not look poisonous, in the phenomenal sense of the term 'look'.

What if 'F' and 'G' are necessarily coextensive? Can something look F without looking G then? The answer again is surely "yes," at least if the necessity is physical. If F-ness is a visual property and G-ness an imperceptible microscopic property nomically correlated with F-ness, something, in looking F, does not look G, in the phenomenal sense of 'looks'.[12]

Consider next the following example: after staring at a green light-bulb, I turn away and I see a large, reddish spot. The spot can look red to me even if I am well aware that there is really no spot present. Can the spot can look red to me without looking disposed to reflect such-and-such percentages of light of so-and-so wavelengths, even if redness is a disposition of this sort?

Clearly, the spot can look *to be* red to me without looking *to be* disposed to reflect such-and-such a percentage of the light, without looking *as if* it is so disposed. Going on the basis of my visual experience, I need not have the slightest inclination to judge anything about light percentages. Epistemic or conceptual 'looks' contexts are hyperintensional in just the way that belief contexts are. Clearly, the spot can also look red, in the phenomenal sense of 'looks', without looking *to have* such and such a light-involving disposition. Again, the latter context is epistemic or conceptual. But if red is a disposition of the above type, then, I maintain, the spot, in looking red, *does* look disposed to reflect such-and-such percentages of the light.

This admittedly sounds strange (and indeed I took the opposing position in my earlier work). But, as Fred Dretske has pointed out to me, the case is parallel to that of seeing John Smith, a policeman, without seeing him to be a policeman. In seeing John Smith, one sees a policeman; one simply fails to recognize *that* he is a policeman. If asked whether one saw a policeman, one will deny it. For one did not know, one had no idea that John Smith was a policeman. Likewise, I suggest, in the above case of phenomenal appearances.

Here is an example[13] that may seem to undercut this position, but which, upon further reflection, actually supports it. I see some square tiles. The tiles look square to me. Square is also the shape of the picture on the wall above the tiles. The light is playing strange tricks so that the tiles do not look to me the shape of the picture. Given that, as I just noted, square *is* the shape of the picture, doesn't this show that phenomenal 'looks' contexts disallow substitutions of coreferential property terms after all?

No, it does not. If the tiles look square to me, and square is the shape of the picture, then, contrary to what is claimed above, the tiles do indeed look the shape of the picture. What the tiles do not look is the shape the picture *looks*. For the light is playing tricks and the picture *looks* some other shape. Once a distinction is drawn between the shape X looks and the (real) shape of X, it seems clearly correct to say that if something Y looks shape S, in the phenomenal sense of 'looks', and S is the (real) shape of X, then Y looks the shape of X.

Further support for the claim that phenomenal 'looks' contexts are *not* intensional to the same degree as propositional attitude contexts comes from the fact that basic experience and feeling are nonconceptual. It seems plausible to suppose that for creatures like us, creatures with an evolutionary history, the phenomenal character of states like feeling pain or having a visual sensation of red is phylogenetically fixed. On this view, through learning we can change our beliefs, our thoughts, our judgments, but not (by and large) how things look and feel (in the phenomenal sense of these terms). Having acquired the concept microscope, say, we can come to see something as a microscope but we do not need concepts simply to see. Once the receptor cells are matured, it suffices to open the eyes. No learning or training is involved. The phenomenal appearances are nonconceptual. Small children see pretty much what the rest of us see. Things look phenomenally to them pretty much as they do to adults. They differ in *how* they see things, in what they see things *as*. They do not see that the kettle is boiling, the house as being dilapidated, the computer as malfunctioning.

Hyperintensionality in belief contexts arises because concepts that necessarily pick out the same property or kind can be different. For example, while it is necessary that water = H_2O, the concept of water is distinct from the concept of H_2O. These distinct concepts afford us two different ways of thinking of a single kind of stuff. Thus, thinking of something as water is different from thinking of it as H_2O. The concepts of water and H_2O share the same referent in all possible worlds (in which they refer) but they deploy different modes of presentation of that referent and thereby they are different concepts.

If indeed, at the phenomenal level, experience is nonconceptual, then it cannot involve or bring to bear concepts or conceptual modes of presentation. So, anyone who takes the view that phenomenal contexts *are* hyperintensional cannot appeal to such modes to explain that level of intensionality.[14]

How, then, is the intensionality of 'looks' talk best explained? The obvious answer surely is that the 'looks' locution, in its phenomenal use, answers to the nonconceptual representational content of the relevant experience. For *X* looks *F* to *S*, in the phenomenal sense of 'looks', just in case *S* undergoes a visual experience with respect to *X* into whose content F-ness enters. Again, the conclusion we naturally reach—given that identity (difference) of phenomenal look goes with identity (difference) of phenomenal character—is that phenomenal character is a species of nonconceptual representational content.

Some philosophers attempt to undercut the above reasoning by denying that 'looks *F*' is to be understood phenomenally, even where '*F*' expresses a property of which one is directly aware via introspection as one undergoes a sensory experience. Ned Block, for example, appeals to the possibility of rife inverted spectra. According to Block (1990), if inverted spectra are rife, blood still looks red to all of us even though widespread phenomenal inversions occur among individual experiences of the color of blood.

Block's argument is unpersuasive. To begin with, the argument does not show that 'looks *F*' never has a purely phenomenal use even if we grant that, where multiple phenomenal inversions occur, blood still looks red to all of us. At best, the argument shows that the 'looks F' locution is not used phenomenally in the case that 'F' is a color term.[15] One can accept this claim while still insisting that 'looks F' has a phenomenal use, where 'F' expresses a property of which one is directly aware in introspecting a sensory experience. For can one maintain, as Shoemaker (1994) does, that our introspective awareness of color is indirect. Moreover, on such a view, the argument from intensionality for representationalism still goes through. What follows is simply that color is not one of the qualities that enters into phenomenal content.

Suppose, for example, that 'R' is a predicate that expresses the property of which I am directly aware in normal perceptual circumstances when I view the apparent color of a ripe tomato. This quality, according to Shoemaker, is not redness. But it is a quality of the tomato. The tomato is R, and it looks R to me. R-ness, on Shoemaker's view, as we will see in detail in chapter 5, is the property of causing a certain intrinsic quality Q of my experience. But, be that as it may, as Shoemaker agrees, the context is intensional. Why? The explanation surely is the same as before: phenomenal character is a matter of representational content. What is now denied is that colors enter into the relevant content.

The second point I want to make about Block's argument is that in the event that inverted spectra are rife, Block is not entitled to assume that blood still looks red to all of us. My intuition is that if we found out that in actual fact inverted spectra are rife, we would want to deny that blood looks red to all of us. To be sure, in this situation blood still looks *like* other red things. For blood looks to each of us the way other red things look. Moreover, there is a shared concept of redness each of us still applies to red things, notwithstanding our phenomenal differences (a concept also possessed by a blind man who believes that fire engines are red, for example), and this concept can be exercised in judgments that things are red made on the basis of how they appear phenomenally. Thus, there is a perfectly good sense in which blood still looks *as if* it is red.[16] But it is *consistent* with these comparative and epistemic claims that blood looks red to some of us, green to others, blue to yet others, and so on. To suppose otherwise is to conflate the phenomenal use of 'looks' with the comparative and/or epistemic uses. Of course, the representationalist needs to be able to give some account of how it *could* conceivably be the case that blood looks red to me and green to you rather than the other way around. But this presents no real difficulty, as I argue in chapter 5.

What goes for 'looks' talk goes for the corresponding talk in connection with perceptual experiences in the other sensory modalities. Intensionality is also found in the case of 'feels' talk and bodily sensations. For example, it can be true that I feel a pain in a leg even if I have had both legs amputated. It can also be true that I feel a pain in a finger without feeling a pain in my mouth even if my finger is in my mouth. These cases again support the representational view of phenomenal character (see Tye 1995 and 1997).

It is sometimes said that even though I can be mistaken about whether I have a limb in which I feel pain and whether I am feeling pain in the place I think I am, I cannot be mistaken about whether I am feeling pain itself. This, it is sometimes alleged, undermines the representational view of pain. For if pain were representational as well as pain location, then misrepresentation ought to be possible with respect the former just as it is with respect to the latter.

My reply is that, on the representational theory, pain is not a mental object that enters into the representational content of the experience of pain. Nor is pain a physical state or property (e.g., tissue damage) that enters into the content. Pain is a feeling.[17] Token pains, accordingly, are token feelings. For example, my pain at time t is one and the same as my feeling or experience of pain at t. That experience, on the representational view, has a representational content that endows it with its phenomenal character. The quality I strongly dislike and of which I am directly aware when I introspect the experience is a quality the experience represents as instantiated in a certain bodily region R. Let us suppose, for purposes of illustration only, that this quality is tissue damage of type T. The experience, then, can go wrong in three ways: (1) there is tissue damage of type T but it isn't located in R, since R does not exist (phantom limb pain); (2) there is tissue damage of type T in some other bodily region but not in region R (referred pain); (3) there is no tissue damage in any bodily location (as, for example, in the case of pain induced by direct cerebral stimulation). In short, on the representational view of pain, there can be both illusions and hallucinations just as in the visual case.

Another objection to the representational approach to the phenomenal character of pain (raised by both Ned Block and John Searle in conversation) is that the possibility of seeing one's damaged leg, say, while one is feeling pain in the leg shows that the phenomenology of the pain experience cannot be captured by its representational content since the content of the perceptual experience, as one views the damaged leg, is the same as, or at least very similar to, the content of the pain experience. Leaving aside the common locational element, however, the phenomenology of the two experiences is radically different.

The mistake here lies in the assumption that the content of the perceptual experience and the content of the pain experience are very similar. What matters to phenomenal character, in my view, is nonconceptual representational content. The perceptual experience nonconceptually represents features such as color, shape, orientation of surface, presence of an edge, and so on. It does not nonconceptually represent tissue damage (or any other comparable quality or cluster of such qualities). Of course, one's damaged leg will look to one *to be* damaged, as one views it. And, of course, it will look *like* a damaged leg. But it will not look damaged *in the phenomenal sense of the term 'looks'*. Thus, the representational theory, far from being embarrassed by the case, actually entails that the phenomenology of the perceptual and pain experiences will be very different.

3.4 PANIC

In the last section, I claimed that phenomenal character is a species of nonconceptual, representational content. In taking this view, I want to emphasize, I am not denying that in some cases conceptualization can *causally influence* phenomenal character. Consider, for example, phenomenal differences in what it is like to hear sounds in French before and after the language has been learned. Obviously there are phenomenal changes here tied to experiential reactions of various sorts associated with understanding the language (e.g., differences in emotional and imagistic responses, feelings of familiarity that weren't present before, difference in effort or concentration involved as one listens to the speaker). There are also phenomenal differences connected to a change in phonological processing. Before one understands French, the phonological structure one hears in the French utterances is fragmentary. For example, one's experience of word boundaries is patently less rich and determinate. This is because some aspects of phonological processing are sensitive to top-down feedback from the centers of comprehension. This feedback enables one to "fill in" the phonetic information (see Jackendoff 1989, p. 99). Still, the influence here is causal, which I am prepared to allow. My claim is that the phenomenally relevant representation of phonological features is nonconceptual, not that it is produced *exclusively* by what is in the acoustic signal.

Likewise, I accept that conceiving of a visual scene or an ambiguous figure in one way rather than another may sometimes influence how we break it up cognitively into spatial parts, for example, and the shapes we then experience may not be the ones we would have experienced under a different conceptualization. Even so, the sensory experiences of shapes (at the most basic level) do not *require* shape concepts. Seeing a cloud, for example, I will likely have an experience of a shape for which I have no corresponding concept.

The same point holds for color. Color experiences, to take one obvious case, subjectively vary in ways that far outstrip our color concepts. For example, the experience or sensation of the determinate shade, red_{29}, is phenomenally different from that of the shade, red_{32}. But I have no such concept as red_{29}. So, I cannot see something as red_{29} or recognize that specific shade as such. For example, if I go into a paint store and look at a chart of reds, I cannot pick out red_{29}. My ordinary color judgments are, of necessity, far less discriminating than my experiences of color.

It will not do to reply that the experience of a particular color shade involves an indexical concept. Which is the relevant concept? It can't be just the concept *that* or *that feature*. In experiencing a particular color, one normally experiences a variety of other features too in the same surface region. Nor can it be the concept *that shade*. Patently, one does not need the concept of a shade to have an experience of one; the same holds for the concept *shade of red*. Nor does it help to appeal to the concept *that color*. Which color? The determinate shade or the general category?

My first condition, then, on the representational content suitable for identification with phenomenal character, is that it be *non-conceptual*, where to say that a mental content is nonconceptual is to say that its subject need not possess any of the concepts that we, as theorists, exercise when we state the correctness conditions for that content.

Another condition is that the relevant content be *abstract*, that is, that it be content into which no particular concrete objects or surfaces enter. This is required by the case of hallucinatory experiences, for which no concrete objects need be present at all; it is also demanded by cases in which different objects look exactly alike phenomenally. What is crucial to phenomenal character is, I claim, the representation of general features or properties.

A third condition is that the content be suitably *poised*. This condition is essentially a functional role one. The key idea is that experiences and feelings, *qua* bearers of phenomenal character, play a certain distinctive functional role. They arise at the interface of the nonconceptual and conceptual domains, and they stand ready and available to make a direct impact on beliefs and/or desires. For example, how things phenomenally look typically causes certain cognitive responses—in particular, beliefs as to how they are if attention is properly focused. Feeling hungry likewise has an immediate cognitive effect, namely, the desire to eat. In the case of feeling pain, the typical cognitive effect is the desire to protect the body, to move away from what is perceived to be producing pain. And so on. States with nonconceptual content that are not so poised lack phenomenal character. Consider, for example, states generated in vision that nonconceptually represent changes in light intensity. These states are not appropriately poised. They arise too early, as it were, in the information processing. The information they carry is not directly accessible to the relevant cognitive centers.

It is worth stressing that, given a suitable elucidation of the "poised" condition, blindsight poses no threat to the representationalist view. Blindsight subjects are people who have large blind areas or scotoma in their visual fields due to brain damage in the postgeniculate region (typically the occipital cortex).[18] They deny that they can see anything at all in their blind areas, and yet, when forced to guess, they produce correct responses with respect to a range of simple stimuli (for example, whether an X or an O is present, whether the stimulus is moving, where the stimulus is in the blind field).

If their reports are to be taken at face value, blindsight subjects do not undergo visual experiences (with respect to their scotoma). They have no phenomenal consciousness in the blind region. What is missing, on the PANIC theory, is the presence of appropriately poised, nonconceptual, representational states. There are nonconceptual states, no doubt representationally impoverished, that make *a* cognitive difference in blindsight subjects. For some information from the blind field does reach the cognitive centers and controls their guessing behavior. But there is no complete, unified representation of the visual field, the content of which is poised to make a direct difference in *beliefs*. Blindsight subjects do not believe their guesses. The cognitive processes at play in these subjects are not belief-forming at all.[19]

Experiences and feelings, then, have poised, abstract, nonconceptual contents. These contents, moreover, may reasonably be called "intentional" in one sense of that term. For, as I urged above, these contents individuate relatively finely (though not as finely as propositional attitude contents). Hence the acronym PANIC: phenomenal character is one and the same as Poised, Abstract, Nonconceptual, Intentional Content. Of course, the term "intentional" is sometimes used to imply that the relevant content is conceptual. In this sense, in my view, phenomenal character is representational but nonintentional.

Which general features enter into *phenomenal contents*, as I shall call them, is not something that can be settled a priori. Empirical investigation is necessary into the functioning of the pertinent sensory systems, and the nature of their output representations. What gets outputted depends upon what gets inputted and how the systems operate. Contents that are poised for us may not be for other creatures and vice versa. This is why we cannot know what it is like to be a bat, for example. Given how we are built, we cannot undergo sensory representations of the sort bats undergo. Consequently, we cannot form phenomenal concepts of the sort available to the bat.

3.5   The Nature of Phenomenal Content

What matters to the phenomenal content of a given state of an individual X is not necessarily any aspect of the actual causal history of X. Intuitively, given the right proximal stimulations, a brain that grows in a vat—a brain that is never properly embodied—has perceptual experiences of features to which it bears no causal connections. What the envatted brain fails to have, intuitively, are *accurate* experiences: things are not as they appear phenomenally to the brain.

The causal connections that matter to phenomenal content, I suggest, are those that *would* obtain, *were* optimal or normal conditions operative. Consider the case of a simple instrument, a temperature gauge, say. When the device is operating normally (when, for example, the tube is fully sealed so that there is a vacuum inside), the height of the mercury column supplies information about the temperature of the surrounding air. In these circumstances, the height of the column causally correlates with, or tracks, temperature. When optimal conditions fail to obtain, the height of the mercury column is no longer a reliable indicator of temperature: misrepresentation can thus occur.

Likewise in the case of experiences. Experiences represent various features by causally correlating with, or tracking, those features under optimal conditions.[20] The brain in the vat has inaccurate perceptual experiences—things are not as they seem—because the brain is not in optimal perceptual conditions and the relevant brain-states are not tracking those features they would track, were optimal conditions to obtain.[21] That perceptually optimal conditions are not met for the brain in the vat seems pretheoretically obvious, however the notion of "optimal conditions" is further spelled out. What counts as optimal conditions and how the tracking relation is to be elucidated are matters that are explored in chapter 6.

The above thesis about phenomenal representation has a subjunctive character. As such, it is not automatically an externalist hypothesis. In this respect, it is like the corresponding thesis for instrument representation. But, evidently, there could be two internally physically identical instruments that were designed for use in very different physical settings and whose internal states tracked different features in those settings, notwithstanding the identity in their 'narrow' behavioral responses to those features. So, externalism is the right view for *some* cases of instrument representation. Unless it can be shown that there is an important disanalogy, the same is true for experiences.

Externalism seems to me plausible for phenomenal representation, where the subject of the experiences is a simple creature having a limited range of behavioral responses and no capacity to introspect its internal states.[22] But it also seems to me the right view to take for the phenomenal representation of color, *if*, as many suppose, color inversion scenarios are metaphysically possible.

The thesis that it is metaphysically possible that there are microphysical twins that differ with respect to the phenomenal character of their inner states (a thesis to which the representationalist is committed if there can be wide phenomenal representation) comports well with the thesis that it is conceptually possible that there are microphysical duplicates that differ phenomenally. The latter thesis, which many philosophers accept, seems very intuitive. It seems no harder to conceive of two creatures, some of whose experiences are phenomenally inverted even though they are physically identical internally, than it is to conceive of two creatures, some of whose experiences are phenomenally inverted even though they are functionally identical. Conceivability does not establish metaphysical possibility, of course. But it is a prima facie warrant for metaphysical possibility. The representationalist has no need to contest the inference in this case. Those who adopt a narrow supervenience thesis with respect to phenomenal character *must* do so (assuming they accept the premise, as, for example, do Block (1990) and Loar (1990).

Before closing this chapter, I want to compare how various theories of phenomenal character do with respect to common philosophical intuitions. As we shall see, representationalism fares extremely well. The intuitions are these:

(1) It is possible for there to be a creature that is a functional duplicate of a sentient being but that lacks any qualia (the Absent Qualia Hypothesis).
(2) It is possible for there to be a creature that is a microphysical duplicate of a sentient being but that lacks any qualia (the Zombie Hypothesis).

(3) It is possible for there to be functional duplicates with inverted qualia (for the case of color, the Inverted Spectrum Hypothesis).

(4) It is possible for there to be microphysical duplicates with inverted qualia.

(5) Qualia are causally efficacious.

In table 3.1, the numbers represent the intuitions, and 'CP' and 'MP' stand for conceptual and metaphysical possibility.

Some clarificatory remarks: (1) I assume that analytic functionalism is wide. Those who deny this should change 2-CP, 2-MP, 4-CP, and 4-MP to "No." (2) The "Yes" in the 1-MP and 3-MP boxes for representationalism reflects the fact that what matters to the relevant sort of representational content is the tracking that *would* obtain *were* optimal conditions operative. Since creatures that are not in optimal conditions but that are, in their given situations, alike with respect to their pattern of causal relations could nonetheless differ with respect to what their inner states would track were optimal conditions to obtain, such creatures could be functional duplicates without being representational duplicates (in one clear sense of the term "functional duplicate").[23] So, on the proposed form of representationalism, there could be absent and inverted qualia. (3) The star in the 5 box for attribute dualism indicates

Table 3.1

	1–CP	1–MP	2–CP	2–MP	3–CP	3–MP	4–CP	4–MP	5
Representationalism of the proposed type	Yes	Yes	Yes	Yes	Yes	Yes	Yes	Yes	Yes
Analytic Functionalism	No	No	Yes	Yes	No	No	Yes	Yes	Yes
Wide functionalism of the empirical type	Yes	No	Yes	Yes	Yes	No	Yes	Yes	Yes
Narrow functionalism of the empirical type	Yes	No	Yes	No	Yes	No	Yes	No	Yes
The Identity Theory	Yes	Yes	Yes	No	Yes	Yes	Yes	No	Yes
Attribute Dualism	Yes	Yes	Yes	Yes	Yes	Yes	Yes	Yes	No*

that the answer is "No" only if another widely accepted thesis is accepted, namely that the physical world is causally closed.

Notes

1. Philosophers who advocate representationalism include Dretske (1995), Harman (1990), Lycan (1996a, 1996b), McDowell (1994), Rey (1992), Tye (1995), and White (1995).

2. Surfaces are not the only particulars we basically see. We also directly see volumes, as, for example, when I view a quantity of Coca-Cola in a glass. For more on surfaces, see chapter 4, note 3.

3. In some cases, it might be replied, you directly experience both qualities that look to you to belong to the surfaces present before you *and* qualities that you experience as being qualities of the visual field, considered as a subjective entity. One such case, according to some philosophers, is that of blurred vision. I am not at all persuaded. For a detailed discussion of blurred vision and other allegedly problematic cases, see chapter 4.

4. Perhaps it will be said that, in attending to the facing surface of something in my field of view—a tomato, say—I am directly aware of the *way* the tomato looks to me. I agree. Intuitively, the way the tomato looks to me is red, and, as I stare at the tomato, I am directly aware of red (or so I claim). For further relevant discussion, see section 3.3 on intensionality.

5. Qualities of sensa are not qualities of experiences, even if it is held that experiences are constituted by both acts of sensing and sensa. To suppose otherwise is to commit a fallacy of composition.

6. For more on this topic, see chapter 7, p. 147.

7. Note that nothing in this appeal rules out a position of the sort endorsed by Shoemaker (1994) wherein phenomenal character is representational content into which certain intrinsic qualities of experience enter. Such a position is indefensible, however, in my view, for other reasons. See chapter 5.

8. In the case of bodily sensations, emotions, and moods, the relevant qualities are qualities of bodily regions, processes, and states.

9. See Dretske (1995).

10. For more on recognitional concepts, see Loar (1990).

11. This is the phenomenological use of the term 'see', not the success use. See chapter 4, p. 83.

12. For a further discussion of cases of this sort and their relevance to causal covariation or 'tracking' accounts of representation, see chapter 6, pp. 139–40.

13. The example is taken from Tye 1995 but the reply to it that follows is opposed to my earlier position.

14. One might here appeal to sensory modes of presentation, that is, to modes that are, in important respects, like conceptual modes but nonetheless nonconceptual. I held this position in Tye 1995. I now think that such an appeal is not sufficiently well motivated, and it introduces unnecessary complexity into the representationalist's position.

15. We can all agree that in some cases 'looks *F*' is not used phenomenally. Consider, for example, 'looks feline', 'looks hungry', 'looks valuable.'

16. This is the sense of 'looks' in which it looks to me as if it is going to rain, as I notice the darkening clouds in the sky.

17. As David Lewis remarks (1983, p. 130), "Surely, that is uncontroversial."

18. See Weiskrantz 1986.

19. Moreover, the impairment in blindsight is not an attentional one. See Tye 1995, appendix.

20. This needs qualification. See chapter 6, pp. 139–40.

21. See ibid.

22. For more here, see chapter 8.

23. I make no claim that this is metaphysically possible for creatures as complex as human beings.

4

Blurry Images, Double Vision, and Other Oddities: New Problems for Representationalism?

In this chapter, I concentrate almost entirely on visual experience and the question of whether there are any clear counterexamples to the following modality-specific, weak representational thesis (R):

Necessarily, visual experiences that are alike with respect to their representational contents are alike phenomenally.

This thesis seems to me to have considerable interest in itself. If it is true, it tells us something important and striking about the metaphysical *basis* of visual phenomenology. If it is false, then strong representationalism—the thesis that phenomenal character is one and the same as representational content that meets certain further conditions—is automatically false, too. At the end of the chapter, I also make some remarks about two examples that purport to show that (R) cannot be strengthened to cover experiences in different sensory modalities that are alike in their representational contents.

The problem cases upon which I am going to focus are all real world ones. So, there is no question about whether the cases *could* occur. Those who think that the inverted spectrum supplies a possible counterexample to (R) will no doubt take the view that this attention to the actual is too confining. After all, (R) is a modal thesis; to refute it, we only need a possible exception.

This is true, of course, as far as it goes. However, if the necessity in (R) is metaphysical, then counterexamples must be metaphysically possible. Mere conceptual possibility will not suffice. Whether the inverted spectrum really does provide metaphysically possible cases of visual experiences that are *phenomenally* inverted and yet *representationally* identical is the topic of the next chapter. My aim in this chapter is more modest: I want to see if any clearcut, actual cases involve representational identity and phenomenal difference.

Christopher Peacocke (1983) adduced a number of interesting examples in which, he claimed, visual experiences have the same representational content but different phenomenal character. I shall have relatively little to say about these examples. Well-known replies to them by representationalists (Harman 1990, DeBellis 1991, Tye 1991) are now available, and I think it is fair to say that a good many philosophers are persuaded by these replies. My primary interest is in a range of new problem cases that have surfaced for thesis (R) in the sixteen years since Peacocke's 1983 was published. The new cases I shall address, though actual, for the most part involve visual *oddities* of one sort or another: blurry images, after-images, phosphenes, tunnel vision, vision with eyes closed, double vision. What I shall try to show is that none of these cases is convincing. Representationalism remains unconquered!

In the first section of this chapter, I sketch out how I think of the various different levels of representational content found in visual experience. In the second section, I take up counterexamples to (R). The final section briefly addresses two problem cases for an amodal version of (R).

4.1   Levels of Content in Visual Experience

Vision is exceedingly complex, too complex to operate all in one stage. It begins with information about light intensity and wavelength at the eye, and ends with a rich and many-layered representation of the visible scene. In between, according to current vision theory, processing occurs in a number of semi-independent modules. According to the version of the story told by David Marr (1982), a primal sketch is first computed for each eye. This representation, which is derived directly from the retinal image, is two dimensional. It specifies the locations of lines and bounded regions of various sorts without any representation of depth. The primal sketch supplies the input to a number of different modules— for example, binocular stereo, structure from motion, and color that together generate a single overall representation of the surfaces and bounded regions present in the given field of view. This latter representation, which Marr calls the *2½-D sketch*, is a vital foundation for further higher level visual processing.

It is now widely accepted in vision theory that a representation similar in character to Marr's 2½-D sketch exists, even though there is substantial disagreement regarding just how this representation is constructed.[1] The relevant representation is usually taken to have a matrix-like structure, the cells of which are dedicated to particular lines of sight.[2] Within each cell are symbols for various local features of any surface at that position in the field of view (for example, distance away, orientation, hue, saturation, brightness, texture, whether a discontinuity in depth is present there, degree of solidity, and so on).[3] Overlaying the matrix are further symbolic representations of edges, ridges, and boundaries.

In some abnormal cases, parts of the structure of the overall representation here—the *grouped, symbol-filled array*, as we might call it (or just the *grouped array*)—are missing. For example, patients with an impairment known as apperceptive agnosia (in the narrow sense)—an impairment typically brought about by damage to the occipital lobes and surrounding regions (typically by carbon monoxide poisoning)—often have roughly normal perception of purely local features in the field of view (for example, color and brightness of local surface patches). But these patients are strikingly impaired in the ability to recognize, match, or even copy simple shapes as well as more complicated figures.[4] In general, they have great difficulty performing any visual tasks that require combining information *across* local regions of the visual field.[5] For example, when shown figure 4.1, one patient consistently read it as 7415.[6] Evidently he was unable to see two parts of a line with a small gap as parts of a single line.[7]

Figure 4.1
The patient read this stimulus as 7415. Reprinted with permission from M. Farah 1990. *Visual Agnosia*, Cambridge, Mass.: MIT Press, p. 14.

Is the content of the grouped array described above actually part of the content of ordinary visual experience? The following example, taken from Irving Rock (1983), may seem to suggest that the answer to this question is "no." The figures in figure 4.2 certainly look different. They continue to look different even if one tilts one's head 45 degrees to the left as one views the right-hand figure, thereby producing exactly the same retinal image as the left-hand figure. Given that the grouped array is a retinotopic representation, its content when one views the right-hand figure (head tilted) is the same as its content when one views the left-hand figure (head upright). But phenomenally there is a clear difference between the two cases.

The phenomenal difference involved in seeing the left-hand figure (head upright) and seeing the right-hand figure (head tilted) is associated

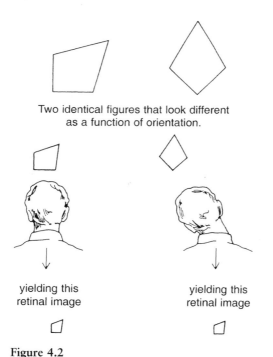

Two identical figures that look different
as a function of orientation.

yielding this   yielding this
retinal image   retinal image

Figure 4.2
The two drawings, although viewed so as to yield identical retinal images, nevertheless look different to naïve observers. Reprinted with permission from I. Rock 1983. *The Logic of Perception*, Cambridge, Mass.: MIT Press.

with the fact that one experiences a very different overall viewer-relative shape in the two cases. (In the one, the experience is of an irregular quadrilateral resting on its side whereas in the other it is of a regular, upright diamond balanced on a point.) What the example really shows, then, is that there are aspects of the content of visual experience that are not captured in the grouped array described above. It does not yet show that the content of the grouped array does not contribute at all to the content of visual experience.

Consider next just the case in which one shifts one's head 45 degrees to the left as one looks at the right-hand figure alone (perhaps closing one's eyes as one does so and reopening them with one's head in the tilted position). I am strongly inclined to think that one's visual experience does not change in any way. There is a change in the content of the retinotopic grouped array, however. It appears, therefore, that the content of the grouped array is indeed not a component part of the content of the visual experience.

Nonetheless, in seeing the world, we certainly have visual experiences as of surfaces and surface details of the sort specified in the grouped array. How can this be? The answer, I suggest, is that, at the level of visual experience, a representation is constructed and deployed with the same general character as the purely retinotopic grouped array but with a more stable content, reflecting a coordinate system whose origin and axes are not fixed relative to the eye alone. In particular, it seems plausible to suppose that while the origin is at the eye, some of the axes (e.g., the up-down axis) are set relative to the body in some way. Given an appropriate coordinate system, the content of *this* grouped array will not alter as one tilts one's head while viewing the right-hand figure. It is, I maintain, at this level, that an array content may be found that is suitable for inclusion in the content of visual experience.

The grouped array—whatever the details of its origin and axes—does not itself yet represent the viewpoint-independent shapes of any objects visible to the viewer (e.g., whether they are rectangles or circles or cubes or spheres). Nor does it classify seen objects into kinds (e.g., tomato, table, etc). Patently, however, our visual experiences do both of these things. We have experiences as of round coins, as of cylindrical locks, and so on. Representations at these levels are also part and parcel of ordinary visual experience. They form further layers of experiential content.

What about the representation of viewer-relative shapes (and other nonlocal spatial properties and relations)? As the example from Rock indicates, that, too, is clearly part of normal visual experience.[8] It is tempting to think that the representation of viewpoint-dependent spatial features does not really form a distinct level from those already differentiated because it seems plausible to claim that once representations in experience are exactly alike with respect to all local features and their grouping, they must be alike with respect to all viewpoint-dependent spatial features of whole surfaces.

The issue is complex, however. Consider an example taken from Peacocke (1992). Suppose that I am looking straight ahead at Buckingham Palace, and then I look at it again with my face still in the same position but with my body turned 45 degrees to the right. The Palace is now experienced as being off to one side from the direction of straight ahead. If the only axis of the relevant grouped array that is set relative to the body rather than the eye is the up-down one, then the content of the grouped array remains constant with the shift in body position. A change with respect to the representation of a viewer-relative spatial property therefore occurs without an accompanying change in the content of the grouped array. Alternatively, if the origin of the grouped array is kept at the eye but *all* of its axes are set relative to the body, then the content of the grouped array changes. On the former proposal, a new layer of content needs to be distinguished for some viewer-relative spatial properties. On the latter, an additional layer of content is not clearly necessary.

I hope that it is evident from my remarks so far that the representational content of visual experience is extremely rich. It operates on a number of different levels and it goes far beyond any concepts the creature may have. Consider, for example, the representation of hue at the level of the grouped array. The fact that a patch of surface is represented in my experience as having a certain hue, red_{19}, say, does not demand that I have the concept red_{19}. For I certainly cannot recognize that hue as such when it comes again. I cannot later reliably pick it out from other closely related hues. My ordinary color judgments, of necessity, abstract away from the myriad of details in my experiences of color. The reason, presumably, is that without some constraints on what can be cognitively extracted, information overload would occur.

Likewise, the representation of viewpoint-relative shape properties is naturally taken to be nonconceptual in some cases. Presented with an unusual shape, I will have an experience of that shape, as seen from my viewpoint. But I need have no concept for the presented shape. I need have no ability to recognize that particular viewer-relative shape when I experience it again. Arguably, even the representation of viewpoint-independent shapes is sometimes nonconceptual.[9] But clearly some representation in visual experience is a conceptual matter (e.g., the representation of object types such as car, ball and telescope).

Some seek to explain the richness of visual experience conceptually by noting that even though the subject often has no appropriate nonindexical concept, he or she is at least aware of the pertinent feature (for example, red$_{19}$, as *that* color or *that* shade or *that* shade of red[10]). As noted in chapter 3, this seems to me unsatisfactory. Intuitively, one can have a visual experience without having such general concepts as *color*, *shade*, or *shade of red*. Indeed, one can have a visual experience without attending to it or its content at all. Moreover, when one does attend, it seems the explanation of one's awareness of the relevant feature as *that* feature is, in part, that one is having an experience that represents it. But no such explanation is possible if the content of the experience is already conceptual.

Given the complexity of the content of visual experience and the number of different channels of information that lie behind its generation, it should not be surprising that in some cases an overall content is produced that is internally inconsistent. An example of this is found in the experience one undergoes as one views the "impossible figure" in figure 4.3 (Gregory 1990, p. 223). One sees each set of stairs as ascending to the next, even though this is impossible. Another example is the waterfall effect, which involves an illusion of movement (originally of a body of water). The most dramatic version of this is obtained by staring at a rotating spiral figure. While rotating, the spiral seems to expand. But after it is stopped, the spiral may seem to contract while nonetheless also seeming not to get any smaller. Again one experiences an impossibility. In this respect, experience is like belief (Harman 1996).

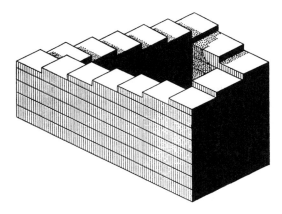

Figure 4.3
The "impossible figure." Reprinted with permission from R. Gregory 1990. *Eye and Brain*, London: Weidenfeld and Nicolson, p. 223.

One further point is perhaps worth making. The term 'experience' can be used in broader and narrower ways. I have assumed in my remarks above that it is correct to say that we have visual experiences as of coins, telescopes, and so forth. Some may prefer to restrict the term 'experience' to states with nonconceptual content, counting the rest as judgments superimposed upon experience proper. This issue seems to me purely terminological. I am here adopting the broader usage, and I shall assume for the purposes of this exposition that the term 'experience' in (R) is to be understood in a broad way. As for the question of which levels of representational content in experience metaphysically determine its phenomenal character, my own view (Tye 1995) is that the relevant levels are nonconceptual, and I shall endeavour to show that the representationalist can account for the problem cases nonconceptually.

So much by way of background on the representational content of visual experience. I turn now to a consideration of counterexamples.

4.2   Replies to Counterexamples

Case 1: The Long, Dark Tunnel
Suppose that you are located in a very dark tunnel, viewing a brightly lit scene at the end. Ned Block (1993, p. 183) has claimed that there will

be a phenomenal difference in your visual experience, if you go from having both eyes open to closing one of them. But, he asserts, the representational content will remain constant: the same objects and properties will be represented.

Reply This is a variant on one of Peacocke's original cases (as Block acknowledges), and I find it no more compelling than its precursor. It seems to me that if there is a genuine phenomenal difference here at all, it *will* be accompanied by a representational difference. In general, using two eyes increases the size of the visual field slightly and thereby increases representational content: more objects or aspects of the brighly lit scene are represented. Hence, the joke by Al Gore that one of the ten best things about being Vice President is that, from the Vice President's chair, if you close your left eye, the seal on the podium in the Senate reads "President of the United States." Using two eyes also improves the perception of depth.

If the tunnel is sufficiently long and dark, there may well be no difference in the representation of depth. In both cases, all the objects in the scene may appear equally distant. But there may still be a small difference in the representation of the periphery of the far end of the tunnel in the two cases or in where the objects are represented as being, relative to one's eyes in the two cases (they may appear to shift in their relative position a little to the left or right). If the viewing situation is such that no changes of this sort occur, then I simply deny that any phenomenal change occurs.

Case 2: The Tilted Coin

A coin is presented at an oblique angle. The coin occupies an elliptical region of the visual field. This is manifest in the experience. But, according to Peacocke (1993), the coin does not look elliptical; it looks circular. The experience represents the coin as circular. In this respect, it is just like the visual experience of the same coin held perpendicular to the line of sight. Phenomenally, however, there is a striking difference.

This case, unlike most of the others in this section, is not a visual oddity but a commonplace occurrence. It is similar to one of Peacocke's original cases (1983) in which two trees of the same size are viewed, one twice as close as the other. Here, if the situation is normal, the visual experience represents the two trees as being the same size. They look to the viewer the same size. But the closer tree occupies a larger region in the visual field, and, in this allegedly nonrepresentational respect, it looks different.

Reply   I begin with the tree example. Here, I claim, the experience represents the nearer tree as having a facing surface that differs in its viewpoint-relative size from the facing surface of the further tree, even though it also represents the two trees as having the same viewpoint-independent size. The nearer tree (or its facing surface) is represented as being *larger from here*, while also being represented as being the same objective size as the further tree. Two different sorts of feature really are being represented, then, although they both are concerned with physical objects (or surfaces).

But what exactly is involved in one of two items being larger from here? The obvious answer is that the one item subtends a larger visual angle relative to the eyes of the viewer. In the case described, it seems plausible to suppose that this is encoded in the relevant visual representation via the greater number of filled array cells devoted to regions of the facing surface of the nearer tree.[11]

It is important to realize that the representation of the relational feature of being larger from here is nonconceptual. For a person to undergo an experience that represents one thing as larger relative to his viewing point than another, it suffices that the encoding feature of the array (larger number of filled array cells) suitably track or causally covary with the instantiation of the viewpoint-relative relation.[12] The person does not need to have any cognitive grasp of subtended angles.

The key claims I want to make, then, with respect to the tree case are these: (1) the nearer tree looks the same objective size as the tree further away while also looking larger from the given viewing position. (2) X looks F to P only if P undergoes a visual experience with respect to X that has a representational content into which F-ness enters. (3) Where the sense of 'looks' in (2) is phenomenal, the representation involved is nonconceptual. (4) The relevant nonconceptual, representational relation is a backward-looking tracking relation. Note that, on this account, the perceiver of the two trees is not the subject of any illusion or error: the nearer tree is just as it looks—both larger from here, the viewing position, and the same viewer-independent size as the tree further away.

Frank Jackson has suggested to me (in correspondence) a simpler reply to Peacocke's tree example. The two trees look the same objective size, but the nearer tree looks nearer. One's experience thus represents the nearer tree as nearer, and this fact suffices to handle the phenomenal difference in one's experience of the two trees. I agree with Jackson that the relative distance away of objects is typically represented in one's visual experiences, but I question whether this line fully captures the intuitive sense in which it is manifest in one's experience that the nearer tree occupies a larger portion of the visual field. After all, if the conditions were atypical and the relative distance away of the two trees were 'lost from one's experience', the nearer tree would still look larger from here (as well as looking objectively larger). And that fact about apparent viewer–relative size remains to be accounted for.

A similar line can be taken with respect to the tilted coin. The coin looks round. It also looks tilted—some parts of its facing surface look nearer than other parts of that surface. The experience thus represents the coin as round, as tilted, and so forth. The coin held perpendicular to the line of sight does not look tilted, however. Therefore, an immediate representational difference exists between the two cases. Furthermore, the tilted coin also looks elliptical from the given viewing position. Here the represented feature is that of having a shape that would be occluded by an ellipse placed in a plane perpendicular to the line of sight. Again the representational is nonconceptual. And again, no illusion is present. The experience is veridical on all levels: the facing surface of the coin really is elliptical from here; the coin really is circular.

Case 3: Blurred Vision

If you unfocus your eyes, you can see objects in a blurry way without seeing them as being blurry. Your experience does not represent the objects as blurry. Representationally, according to Boghossian and

Velleman (1989), your experience after you unfocus your eyes is the same, in all salient respects, as the experience before. But, phenomenally, there is a difference. A similar case is raised by Block (as yet unpublished). He asks us, first, to imagine that we are watching a movie screen that fills our whole field of vision. The images on the screen are themselves blurry and look that way. Here Block claims we have clear impressions of blurry images. In a second example, we are reading a program in the movie theater and we then look up at the screen. The images on the screen now may or may not be blurry (as far as we are aware), but we have a blurry impression of them. Block is dubious that the representationalist can capture this difference satisfactorily.

Another everyday example worth mentioning is that of poor eyesight. When I take off my my reading glasses, my vision of nearby things blurs a little. Alternatively, if I stare at a bright light and look away, I have a blurry or fuzzy afterimage. Blurriness, it might be claimed, is an aspect of the phenomenal character of my visual experiences in both of these examples that is not fixed by the representational content of the experiences.

Reply   There is indeed *a* difference between the case of seeing objects blurrily and the case of seeing them as blurry. Properly understood, however, this is no threat to the representationalist's position. When one sees a sharp object *as* blurry, one sees it as having indistinct contours and boundaries. This, we can agree, is not what normally happens when one unfocuses one's eyes or takes off one's eye glasses. In these cases, one simply loses information. Likewise, when one sees the world through eyes that are half closed. In seeing blurrily, one undergoes sensory representations that fail to specify just where the boundaries and contours lie. Some information that was present with eyes focused is now missing. In particular, the grouped array contains less definite information about surface depth, orientation, contours, and so forth.

In the case of squinting, I might add, even though information is lost, one can sometimes come to see something one couldn't see before. For example, when one squints at figure 4.4 from a distance, one reduces the amount of information one has about the sharp edges of the blocks. Since

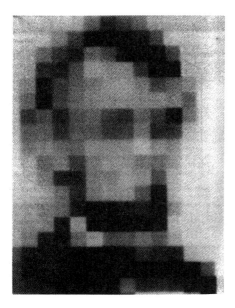

Figure 4.4
A checkerboard picture devised by Leon D. Harmon. It should be viewed at a distance through half-closed eyes. Reprinted with permission from L. D. Harmon, 1973. The recognition of faces, *Scientific American*, November, p. 75.

representation of the sharp edges interferes with some of the processing that generates representation of large-scale features, the latter actually becomes more efficient during squinting, with the result that one is now able to recognize that the figure is Abraham Lincoln.

To return to blurred vision, in the case of seeing sharp objects as blurry, one's visual experience comments inaccurately on boundaries. It 'says' that the boundaries themselves are fuzzy when they are not. In the case of seeing blurrily, one's visual experience does not do this. It makes no comment on where exactly the boundaries lie. Here there is no inaccuracy.

There is a further difference between the two cases. When one sees an object or screen image itself as blurry, one brings to bear a conceptual representation of blurriness, a representation that demands that one have a cognitive grasp of what it is for something to have indistinct or fuzzy boundaries. By contrast, in the case of seeing something blurrily, the representation is nonconceptual. A small child with poor eyesight can see things blurrily. Also, a small child with good eye sight can see blurry things clearly. That too is nonconceptual. A threefold distinction thus emerges: seeing as blurry, seeing blurrily, and seeing clearly something blurry. Only the first of these involves a conceptual representation of blurriness.

The difference, I might add, between seeing a blurry screen image *blurrily* and seeing that same screen image *clearly* has to do with the degree of representational indeterminacy in the experience. In seeing the image blurrily, one's experience is less definite about boundaries and surface details than the blurriness in the image warrants. In seeing the same screen image clearly, one's experience accurately captures the image blurriness.

Still, is there really any *phenomenal* difference between seeing blurrily and seeing as blurry or between seeing blurrily a clear thing and seeing clearly a blurry thing? To be sure, there is a difference in higher-order consciousness between realizing that one is seeing blurrily and realizing that one is seeing as blurry, but this is extrinsic and nonphenomenal. There is also normally an associated phenomenal difference connected with the presence of characteristic bodily sensations involved in the region of the eyes when one sees blurrily (one's eyes 'feel' different). And seeing as blurry may well be accompanied by a linguistic, auditory image of oneself saying (in one's native tongue) that the relevant thing is blurry. That image, like other images, will have phenomenal features. But leaving these differences aside, is there any inherent phenomenal difference between the two states in typical cases, or between the states of seeing a clear thing blurrily and seeing a blurry thing clearly?

It seems obvious that, in principle, an experimental setup could be devised that would leave one without any way of telling from the phenomenal character of one's visual experience (*without any additional cues*) whether one had shifted from seeing a sharp screen image through a blur to seeing clearly a suitably blurred version of that same screen image in at least some cases. Still, there does seem to me a purely visual phenomenal difference in some cases too.

Here is an example from Frank Jackson that illustrates the point. Consider a watercolor painting done on wet paper so that the edges of the colored shapes blur. If I view such a painting with my glasses on, I have a clear impression of a blurry representation. Now consider a watercolor painting done on dry paper with sharp edges to the colored shapes. Viewing a painting of this sort with my glasses off, I have a blurry impression of a clear representation. Typically, there is a phenomenal difference between the two cases.

Jackson agrees with me that this example presents no problem for representationalism, however. His suggestion (in correspondence) is that with the blurry watercolor, my visual experience represents quite precisely the blurriness of the edges; that is, it represents (a) that the edges definitely fall between spatial regions A and B of the paper and (b) that it is indefinite exactly where between A and B on the paper the edges fall. With the clear watercolor, seen without eye glasses, my visual experience is silent on the precise locus of the edges; that is, my experience represents that the edges of the colored shapes definitely fall between A and B while failing to represent exactly where it is between A and B the edges lie.

What about the example of the fuzzy afterimage? When one sees an afterimage, there is nothing that one sees. The term 'see' here has a phenomenal sense that lacks existential import. It is the sense that is operative when we say that Macbeth saw a dagger. Seeing a blue, circular afterimage consists in having a certain kind of visual experience. The experience isn't blue or circular. Rather, it is an illusory experience as of something blue and circular (from here), something filmy and hovering in space.[13] The fuzziness of the afterimage is, I suggest, a straightforward reflection of the representational impoverishment of the relevant visual experience. The experience does not "say" where the boundaries of the nonexistent blue, circular thing lie. Again, no difficulty for representationalism.

Case 4: The Apparent Location of an Afterimage

A flashbulb goes off. You see a red afterimage in front of a photographer's face. You are under no illusion about what you are seeing. You are well aware that the spot you see is an afterimage. According to Boghossian and Velleman (1989), you do not see the afterimage as actually existing in front of the photographer's face. Rather, you see it as a spot that appears there. The afterimage *appears to you in* a certain location without *appearing to you to be in* that location. Nothing appears to be in the location in question. The representational content of your experience is (in part) that there is nothing between you and the photographer. Even so, the difference phenomenologically between this case and that in which you experience the photographer's face without a red afterimage in front of it is vast. This difference can only be accounted for, Boghossian and Velleman claim, by reference to a sensory field with intrinsic sensational qualities instantiated in portions of it.

In the case of the color of the afterimage, according to Boghossian and Velleman, the situation is a little different. For here, they maintain, you can see the afterimage not just as appearing red but as *being* red. Assuming that your experience is veridical—you see the afterimage as an afterimage—a further difficulty now arises. What does your experience represent as actually being red? Not any external object (for that would make the experience illusory, which, by hypothesis, say Boghossian and Velleman, it is not), nor the image itself. On the representationalist view, there is no image in the content of the experience. Once again, it seems that we need to concede that the phenomenology isn't fixed by the representational content. Redness doesn't enter into the content. Rather, phenomenal or sensational redness is a feature of a portion of the *sensory* field.

Reply   This conclusion is one we would do well to avoid. For one thing, it smacks of the classical sense-datum theory. For another, colors can certainly be seen as belonging to things in the environment. So, unless in all cases the colors we see are really properties of our visual fields,[14] we face a very puzzling question: How can a portion of a visual field, understood now as a subjective entity, share a property with something objective in the external environment?

Happily, the representationalist need not be concerned with these matters. In my view, there is a clear sense in which the basic experiences involved in seeing afterimages are *always* illusory; for when one sees an afterimage, there is nothing that one sees. As noted earlier, the term 'see' in this context has a phenomenal sense; it is not a success verb. There is also a sense in which some afterimage experiences are veridical since one can indeed see an afterimage as an afterimage. In so doing, one makes no mistake, any more than does the person who hallucinates a pink elephant and who sees the hallucinated elephant as not really existing. The spot one apprehends, like the elephant, is unreal.[15] If the subject of the afterimage experience grasps this fact, he can conceptually represent the spot *as* unreal. And that conceptualization can enter into his overall experience, broadly understood. But the fact that some afterimage experiences are veridical in the latter sense clearly does not threaten the claim that they are all illusory in the former sense. Once this is admitted, no good reason remains to deny that when one sees a red afterimage, redness enters into the content of the experience.

Turning now to the example of apparent location, consider first the case in which one sees a red afterimage in front of a much larger background yellow surface without realizing that it is an afterimage. Here one undergoes an illusory experience as of something red and filmy hovering in space in front of something yellow—an experience similar perhaps to that of viewing (in dim lighting) a blood stain on a transparent sheet of glass suspended between oneself and a yellow background surface. Now suppose that one realizes that one is having an afterimage. One is no longer inclined to believe that there is something red suspended in space before one. Nonetheless, at the *nonconceptual* level, one still undergoes an experience as of something red in front of a yellow background. At this level, one's experience is still phenomenally similar to the veridical experience of the blood stain. That this is so, if anyone has any doubt, is shown by the fact that even if one is firmly convinced that one is having an afterimage, one can be mistaken.[16] But conceptually, things are now different. One now sees the spot one is experiencing as unreal, as not actually being in front of a yellow surface at all.

Accordingly, a conflict obtains between the nonconceptual and the conceptual contents of the experience. In the nonconceptual sense, the afterimage appears in front of a yellow surface. This is the sense of 'appears' that goes with the nonconceptual, phenomenal sense of 'see'. Even though the spot does not exist, one sees it; and one sees the spot just in case it appears some way. Since one sees what does not exist only if one is subject to an illusory experience, appearing at this level is certainly a function of the content of the experience. But it is not dependent upon the concepts one possesses. Although the afterimage nonconceptually appears in front of a yellow surface, it does not appear *to be* there. Indeed, it appears *not* to be there. This is the conceptual or epistemic sense of appearing.[17] In general, *x* appears *to be F* to *P* only if *X* possesses the concept *F* (just as *P* sees *x* as *F* only if *P* possesses the concept *F*). The afterimage experience overall, then, has a content that is necessarily inconsistent. In this respect, it is like experiences of impossible figures (such as figure 4.3).

One way to think about this case is to imagine a witness at a trial telling her account of events on some past evening. The judge hears the witness but he has conflicting information from other sources he finds more compelling. So, he does not believe her; indeed, he believes that what she says is false. The subject of the afterimage experience in the above example is comparable to the judge here. The former, like the latter, makes a higher-level "assessment" based on her overall information that is at odds with a lower-level "report" she has.[18] Both the "report" and the "assessment" enter into the afterimage experience, broadly understood.[19]

Many examples exist of similar nonconceptual/conceptual conflicts in experience. If I find out that I am viewing a *trompe l'oeil* painting of a garden of flowers through a window and not a real garden and window as I had supposed, I may come to see what is before my eyes as a clever two-dimensional piece of trickery while still having a visual experience that nonconceptually represents brightly colored items at varying distances away.[20]

Case 5: Eyes Closed toward the Sun

This example is again from Peacocke (1993). Close your eyes and look toward the sun. Likely, you'll experience swirling shapes. But phenomenally, your experience isn't really like visual experiences you undergo of moving shapes in your environment. This case can be viewed as a challenge to the advocate of (R) to say what is different about the representational content of the experience, eyes closed, that determines the different phenomenal character.

Block (1996) has a similar example that involves phosphene experiences. Push your eyeballs in for about a minute. You'll experience bright changing colors. But your experience, Block claims, isn't representational.[21] If this is correct, then phenomenally different phosphene experiences have the same representational content, namely none, and (R) is false.

Reply Representations are typically indeterminate with respect to some aspects of the things they represent. If, for example, I say to you, "There's a tall man at the door," my assertion leaves open whether he is wearing a hat, the look on his face, whether he is overweight, and many other features. It simply does not comment on these matters. Likewise, if I draw a picture of the man, I may well leave unspecified how many stripes are on his shirt, the color of his cheeks, whether he is wearing a belt. In the case where I experience swirling shapes, there is also representational indeterminacy.

Consider again the earlier example of the tilted coin. Here my experience represents the coin as having certain viewpoint-independent and viewpoint-dependent properties—as being both round and elliptical from here, for example. My experience conceptually classifies it as a public object and as a coin, in particular. When I experience swirling shapes with my eyes closed, my experience is representationally much more impoverished. It does not conceptually represent that a public object is present. Indeed, there is no representation, conceptual or nonconceptual, of viewpoint-independent properties or of the third spatial dimension. There is representation only in two dimensions and only at the level of the grouped array. Bounded spatial regions are delineated; certain local features are specified—for example, color. Thereby certain irregular, viewpoint-dependent, shape features are represented. But the representation goes no further; it makes no further comment.

Of course, on this account, the experience of swirling shapes is inaccurate or illusory. What it 'says' is not the case. No items are present with the relevant viewer-relative shapes. But this surely is no problem. Given the abnormality of the sensory situation, error is to be expected.

A parallel response can be made to the phosphene case. Again, one's experience is highly indeterminate representationally. But intuitively there is *some* content there. As Harman (1996) notes, the phosphene experience has a phenomenal character rather like those one undergoes viewing the end of a fireworks show or during the light displays in some rock concerts. The relevant content, then, is plausibly taken to be similar to the nonconceptual content that is present in the latter cases. The main difference is that in the phosphene case, one's experience is illusory: the correctness conditions are not satisfied.

Perhaps it will be said that in both the phosphene case and that of the swirling shapes, one sees the moving expanses as unreal, as not actually being in public space at all. So, there is representation beyond the level of the grouped array. That seems to me not obvious. What *is* obvious is that one does not see the expanses as actually being in public space since that is not how one typically conceives of the expanses in such experiences. But even if one does see the expanses as unreal, there is no pressing difficulty. The experiences now have a conceptual layer of content that is inconsistent with the nonconceptual one, just as in case 4.

The upshot, I suggest, is that the above examples present no immediate difficulty for representationalism.

Case 6: Double Vision

Boghossian and Velleman (1989, p. 94) have one further case worth mentioning:

If you press the side of one eyeball, you can see this line of type twice without seeing the page as bearing two identical lines of type. Indeed, you cannot even force the resulting experience into representing the existence of two lines, even if you try. Similarly, you can see nearby objects double by focusing on distant objects behind them, and yet you cannot get yourself to see the number of nearby objects as doubling.

The conclusion they draw is that experiences such as these cannot be described correctly in terms of their intentional content alone.

Reply I am not persuaded. It is certainly the case that when one presses one's eyeball, one has no inclination to think or judge that the number of lines of type has doubled. After all, the duplicate line is fainter than the original, and one knows full well what one is doing. So, in the epistemic or conceptual sense of the term 'appears', it does not appear that the number of lines has doubled. It does not look as if the number of lines has doubled. But phenomenologically, there is, of course, a conspicuous change. This, the representationalist can plausibly claim, is because at the level of the grouped array, there is a change in representational content. The surface that is identified within the overall experience as the page now has small regions represented as black that were represented as white before (corresponding to those places where one sees the duplicate line).[22]

Where this case differs from that in which one sees two identical lines of type *as* two such lines (leaving aside the issue of faintness) is in a much higher conceptual layer of content. In the latter case, unlike the former, one brings to bear the complex concept *two lines of type* in one's experience. So, once again, no representational identity.[23] Likewise for the case of seeing double and seeing as two *simpliciter*: A small child who cannot count to two and so cannot see *as* two can still see double.

The fact that seeing double is a representationally distinct state from seeing two things as two does not entail that the two states are *inherently* phenomenally different. After all, it is surely the case that an experimental set-up could be produced that adjusted for the faintness usually associated with seeing double and left one unable to say, from the phenomenal character of one's visual experience *alone*, whether one had shifted from seeing one thing double to seeing two things accurately or vice-versa, just as in the earlier example of blurry vision.[24]

Case 7: Sexism, Racism, and Ageism

Most men and nearly all women have normal color vision, as measured by standard color tests such as those of Ishihara and Farnsworth. But people vary according to gender, race, and age in their performance in matching experiments. For example, when subjects are shown a screen, one half of which is lit by a mixture of red and green lights and the other by yellow or orange light, and they are asked to adjust the mixture of lights so as to make the two halves of the screen match in color, they disagree about the location of the match. Where one male subject sees the two sides of the screen as being the same in color, a female subject may see one side as a little redder or greener. Corresponding differences occur with age and race as well.

In a recent article (1999a), Block claims that "(t)he fact that people match differently gives us reason to suppose that the phenomenal character of an experience of a narrow shade—say a specific Munsell chip—may not be the same for any two persons if they differ in sex, race, or age." There is no difference in the representational content of the shade experiences of the same Munsell chip, however, if the perceivers are normal, according to Block. For if there were, then some shade experiences of normal perceivers would be inaccurate. And that, Block maintains, just isn't plausible: there is no privileged class of *normal* perceivers. To say that the men track the shades accurately and the women do not is sexist. To prefer the young to the old is ageist. To suppose whites get it right and blacks do not is racist. But if phenomenal difference obtains without representational difference, then thesis (R) is false.

To see what is wrong with this argument, consider two normal perceivers, Ted and Alice, both of whom are looking at a Munsell chip M in ideal viewing circumstances. Let us grant that their color experiences are veridical. Suppose that there is a mixture of colored lights, the shade of which Ted exactly matches to the shade of M but which Alice distinguishes from it, matching instead the shade of that mixture of lights to a different Munsell chip. Alice, thus, makes a finer discrimination than Ted—evidence of a phenomenal difference in their experiences of M.

It may seem that there is room for another possibility here. Suppose that the mixture of lights is not the same shade as M at all, but a distinct shade that Ted cannot distinguish from the shade of the chip whereas Alice can. In this case, it may be suggested, the phenomenal character of their shade experiences of M is the same while the phenomenal character of their shade experiences of the mixture of lights is different.

The root problem with this proposal is that phenomenal differences are accessible to appropriately attentive subjects. If the phenomenal character of Ted's shade experience of M were different from that of his shade experience of the mixture of lights, then that difference, however small, would be reflected in Ted's judging that M and the mixture of lights do not quite match shadewise. But ex hypothesi, Ted judges, on the basis of his experiences, that the two *do* match with respect to shade. So, for Ted, there is no difference in phenomenal character: M and the mixture of lights look phenomenally the *same* shade to him. On the representationalist view, then, Ted visually represents M and the mixture of lights as having the same shade. Since Ted's experience is veridical, it follows that M and the mixture of lights have the same shade, contrary to the initial supposition.

The representationalist, thus, should hold that the phenomenal character of Ted's experience of chip M is indeed different from that of Alice's experience of M. M looks a certain shade—call that shade S—to Ted and it also looks a certain shade—call it S'—to Alice. M looks the same shade as the mixture of lights to Ted, but the mixture of lights looks a different shade (S'') to Alice (that of another chip). If, as the representationalist maintains, phenomenal difference requires representational difference, then the shades Ted and Alice visually represent the chip M as having are different. Given that both Ted and Alice have veridical experiences, it follows, on the representationalist view, that the chip is S *and* S', where S is not identical with S'. How can this be? How can a single chip (or, for that matter, a single mixture of lights) have multiple shades?

The answer, of course, is that something can have two or more shades so long as at least one of the shades is nonminimal, where a *minimal* shade is one for which there is no *other* shade that is a shade of it. For example, scarlet is a shade of red. Bright scarlet is a shade of scarlet. One and the same entity can be both bright scarlet and scarlet since at least one of these shades is nonminimal. (In fact, both are).

Consider, then, shades S and S'. The chip viewed by Ted and Alice can have both shades since (at least) S is nonminimal. S' is a shade of S that Ted fails to discriminate. Alice picks out S', since she has a more sensitive shade detector than Ted. Her color vision is attuned to more subtle variations in shade than Ted. Neither has an inaccurate color experience, however.

Here is a parallel. Suppose that I have a scale at home for weighing myself. The scale is calibrated in single units. When I stand on it, it reads

162. In the doctor's office, on the same morning, I am weighed again. His scale is more finely calibrated. It reads 162 1/8. On the same scale, a little later, having eaten a snack, I am weighed once more. The reading is now 162 3/8. If my home scale still reads 162 when I stand on it, then there is a difference in my weight that my home scale fails to register. But that doesn't make it inaccurate. Given its design, it is merely a less sensitive representational device than the scale used by my doctor.

Of course, the reply I have given to Block's argument requires the assumption that things can have shades that *some* normal perceivers fail to discriminate even in ideal circumstances. And some philosophers will reject this assumption. But on an objectivist conception of color (see chapter 7), it seems unproblematic. Take another perceptual case, that of depth vision. Obviously even among normal perceivers, there are subtle differences in the distance away of objects that are discriminable only to some of the perceivers. Some normal perceivers have more sensitive (more finely calibrated) depth detectors than others. Likewise in the case of shades of color.

Block also discusses the case of color experiences that differ among normal perceivers at a less fine-grained level. Something that looks more red than orange to me may look more orange than red to you; something that I experience as unique green, you may experience as green with a tinge of blue. How can this be, on a representationalist account, if we are both undergoing veridical color experiences?[25]

The first point to make by way of reply is that there are visual representations both of colors and of (more or less narrow) shades. Since colors comprise or include many shades, in representing something X as having a certain color, my experience effectively classifies it along with many other things whose color shades I can discriminate from X. Such classifications will certainly vary somewhat from person to person, and these classifications will be reflected in differences in verbal and nonverbal behavior in certain situations. Given these differences, there is no difficulty in allowing that a thing can be both more red than orange (for me) and more orange than red (for you). For it suffices that the red (orange) classifications at play in our experiences range over slightly different sets of shades. If a shade in my category of red is in your category of orange, something can look more red than orange to me while looking more orange than red to you. And we can both be right. Likewise, for the case of unique green and green tinged with blue.

It is worth stressing that the above talk of visual classifications and categories need not be taken to commit the representationalist to the view that the representation of colors, as opposed to shades, in visual experience always involves the application of color concepts. To be sure, the classifications typically elicit conceptual responses. But it is open to the representationalist to argue that just as it is possible for a visual experience to represent something as having a certain fine-grained shade without the subject of the experience applying a concept to that shade, so too is it possible for the case of color. If the visual system is set up so that experiences "track" colors in the appropriate conditions, they can thereby represent the colors, whether or not the subjects extract that information and use it in their beliefs.

4.3   Crossmodal Cases

In this section, I want to discuss two cases that involve different sensory modalities. These cases purport to refute the following thesis:

(R′) Necessarily, perceptual experiences that are alike with respect to their representational contents are alike phenomenally.

Once again, I shall argue, the representationalist has plausible replies.

The first example is from Block (1995). It compares having a visual experience as of something overhead versus having an auditory experience as of something overhead. Block claims that this example shows that there are phenomenal differences that are not representational. Supposedly, there is *no* common phenomenal quality to these experiences, even though they overlap representationally.

In Tye (1995), I pointed out that it isn't obviously true that there is no phenomenal overlap. What is obviously true is that the look and the sound phenomenally differ. In his original discussion, Block says that in the case he has in mind, one only catches a glimpse so that "the (phenomenal) difference cannot be ascribed to further representational differences" (1995, section 4.2). So understood, the case is a putative counterexample to (R′).

However, even if one only has a glimpse, other features will inevitably be represented in the one experience that are not represented in the other. For example, in the case of the auditory experience, one is bound to have some impression of how loud the sound is. One will also normally have some visual impression of the thing's color and viewer-relative size (whether or not one notices these features—that is, whether or not one conceptually represents them in one's experience). And those won't be represented in the auditory experience.

Block (1996) now claims that in his original example he had in mind peripheral vision of movement in which there is no representation of color, size, or shape. The content is just that something is moving over there. But he now concedes that in the auditory experience, there will inevitably be representation of how loud the sound is. He remarks:

> That does not ruin the point. It just makes it harder to see. Imagine the experience of hearing something and seeing it in your peripheral vison. It is true that you experience the sound as having a certain loudness, but can't we abstract away from that, concentrating on the perceived location? And isn't there an obvious difference between the auditory experience *as of that location* and the visual experience *as of that location*? (1996, p. 38)

His conclusion is that representationally identical experiences in different sensory modalities can differ phenomenally.

I find myself quite perplexed by these remarks. How are we meant to abstract away from the loudness of the sound and focus on the perceived location in the auditory case? After all, as Block grants, we have no auditory experiences that are not as of sounds. Nor can we even imagine having any such experiences (at least I can't). So, it seems to me, we do not have the faintest idea what such experiences are supposed to be like. Perhaps what Block means us to do is to mentally block out the sound in the auditory experience. But now it seems to me not at all obvious that the experience that remains accessible to us is any different phenomenally from the visual one of movement alone (assuming we also mentally block off any further information in the visual experience about the background colors, shapes, and so forth).

The second example is one of seeing a round shape and feeling that shape by running one's fingers over it.[25] Suppose that in both cases, one has an experience as of a round shape. Still, the one is a haptic experience and the other a visual experience. Phenomenologically, there is a large difference between the two—a difference (according to some) that (R') cannot account for.

One obvious immediate reply the representationalist can make is that in seeing the shape, one has an experience as of color. But color isn't represented in the content of the haptic experience. Conversely, temperature is represented in the haptic experience but not in the visual one (or at least not to the same extent). Likewise, there is much more detailed representation of degree of solidity in the haptic experience. Another representational difference pertains to the location of the shape. In vision, the shape is automatically represented as having a certain two-dimensional location relative to the eyes. It is also normally represented as being at a certain distance away from the body. In the haptic case, however, shape is represented via more basic touch and pressure representations of contours derived from sensors in the skin. Here the shape is represented as belonging to a surface with which one is in bodily contact. Moreover (and relatedly) in the haptic experience, there is no representation of the shape's two-dimensional location relative to the eyes. Finally, and very importantly, in the visual case, there is representation not only of viewer-independent shape but also of viewer-relative shape (e.g., being elliptical from here). The latter property, of course, is not represented in the haptic experience.

Perhaps it will be replied again that we can abstract away from *all* these differences and focus on the representation of shape itself. Having done so, we will still be left with an obvious phenomenal difference between the visual experience as of a round shape and the haptic experience as of that shape. I can only say again that this seems to me not in the least obvious. Indeed, it is hard to make sense of the idea that via such a process of mental abstraction, we are left with any distinctively visual or haptic experiences to focus on at all.

That completes my survey of problem cases. The onus now rests with opponents of representationalism to find other more compelling counterexamples. Given the richness of the content of perceptual experience, I am very doubtful that such counterexamples will be forthcoming either to (R) or to (R').

Notes

1. This representation is sometimes supposed to occur in a medium shared with imagery; see Kosslyn (1994).

2. The matrix or array cells need not be physically contiguous at all. Instead, like the arrays found inside computers, they can be widely scattered. What is crucially important is that cells representing adjacent regions of the visual field be operated upon by routines that treat those cells as if they were adjacent; see Tye (1991 and 1995).

3. The notion of a surface here is to be understood broadly. A flickering flame, for example, has a constantly changing surface in the relevant senses of 'surface'. A cloud has a surface, as does a spray of water. Glowing matter from exploding fireworks has brightly colored surfaces. There are no immaterial surfaces, however. In the relevant sense, surfaces are always public, physical entities.

4. Movement of shapes sometimes helps these patients to identify them; see, for example, Efron (1968), p. 159.

5. They do better at identifying real objects (e.g., toothbrushes, safety pins) than simple shapes. However, their improved performance here is based on *inferences* from clues provided by color, texture, and so forth.

6. The patient made this identification by tracing around the figure with movements of his hand and relying on local continuity. See T. Landis et al. (1982).

7. It has been suggested that the visual experiences of these patients are something like those you or I would undergo if we donned masks with a large number of pin holes in them.

8. Indeed a critical part, as we'll see later.

9. See Peacocke (1993) for some plausible examples.

10. See McDowell (1994).

11. For more on this subject, see Tye (1996c). For an alternative reply, see Lycan (1996a). This reply is criticized in Tye (1996c).

12. This oversimplifies minimally. For a qualification and a fuller account of nonconceptual representation, see Tye (1995 and 1998a).

13. Not everyone accepts that such experiences are always illusory. See the next case.

14. This highly counterintuitive position is adopted by Boghossian and Velleman (1989). In their view, we mistakenly project colors onto external things.

15. Its status is that of an intentional inexistent, like that of the eternal life some hope for or the golden fleece Jason sought. (In saying this, I do not mean to suggest that we need to quantify over intentional inexistents).

16. A famous psychological experiment is worth mentioning here. It does not involve afterimages but it does bring out how mistakes can be made about whether one is imaging something or actually seeing it (in the success sense of 'see'). In the

experiment, subjects in a room with normal lighting were asked to face a screen and to imagine a banana on it. Unknown to the subjects, a projector was set up behind the screen containing a slide of a banana. Once the subjects reported that they had formed their images, the illumination on the projector was slowly increased so that it eventually cast a picture of a banana on a screen that was clearly visible to any newcomer entering the room. However, none of the subjects ever realized that they were looking at a real picture. Instead, they noticed merely that their "images" changed in certain ways—for example, orientation—as time passed. For more on this experiment, see Perky (1910).

17. For more here, see Jackson (1977) and Dretske (1995).

18. One possible relevant piece of information here concerns the way in which the afterimage moves with the movement of the eyes.

19. Of course, the "report" in the afterimage case isn't conceptual. In this important respect, it differs from the report the judge hears from the witness.

20. In my discussion of case 4, I have spoken as if afterimages are one and the same as certain unreal, intentional objects. In the final analysis, I am inclined to reject this unqualified view, since it entails that afterimages are not mental entities (any more than are centaurs and unicorns). Another related problem is that the position produces a lack of systematic unity in the treatment of so-called "phenomenal objects." For pains, itches, and tickles are surely mental (and necessarily private). On my present view, the term 'afterimage' is ambiguous. Sometimes it refers to a visual experience; sometimes it picks out an intentional object. For more on the former usage and the reasons for supposing that afterimages are visual experiences, see Tye (1995).

21. Or may not be. Block (p. 35) hedges a bit.

22. Of course, I am using the term 'see' here in the phenomenological sense.

23. Is it possible to see the number of things as doubling while also seeing double? Yes. Suppose one is viewing a movie screen on which the number of images doubles every ten seconds until the screen is full, and then the doubling process starts anew. One is aware that this is going on and one sees the number of images as doubling. After a while, one starts to drink alcohol, with the result that one comes to see individual images double. One is now seeing double while also seeing the number of screen images itself as doubling.

24. Paul Boghossian has commented to me that the case of ambiguous figures presents a further problem for those representationalists who want to claim that phenomenal character is identical with or fixed by nonconceptual representational content. For a discussion of ambiguous figures and a defense of representationalism here, see Tye (1995), pp. 140–41.

25. This case was raised at the 1995 SOFIA conference in Cancun, the proceedings of which are published in *Philosophical Issues* 7, 1996. It has also come up several times in conversation.

5

On Moderation in Matters Phenomenal: Shoemaker and Inverted Qualia

One reaction some philosophers have to the representational view of experience is that it does not accomodate satisfactorily the intuition that the phenomenal character we are confronted with in perceptual experience is due not just to what is out there but also to us, to our own internal physiological make-up. Hence the apparent coherence of inverted spectra scenarios. This reaction, in some cases, leads to an outright rejection of the representational approach to phenomenal character.[1] In the case of Sydney Shoemaker, however, it has led to the proposal of a complex, mixed account of phenomenal character that is intended to do justice to the phenomenology by appealing to represented qualities while also preserving a place for intrinsic qualities of experience.[2]

I have two aims in this chapter. First, I want to show that Shoemaker's hybrid position—moderate representationalism, as we might call it—encounters a number of very serious problems. Second, I want to take a close look at the sorts of inverted spectrum scenarios that Shoemaker's account is intended to cover. What I shall argue is that, properly understood, none of them create trouble for the pure representationalist.

5.1 A Critique of Shoemaker's Theory

I begin with a brief summary of Shoemaker's view. Suppose that Jack and Jill are both normal perceivers viewing a ripe tomato in good light. Neither one is misperceiving its color. Still, according to Shoemaker, the possibility remains that their color experiences are phenomenally inverted—that the phenomenal character of their experiences is radically different. In this situation, Jack and Jill both have a visual experience that represents the tomato as red. However, when they introspect, the qualities of which they are introspectively aware, Shoemaker maintains, are qualities of the tomato. For Shoemaker accepts the claim that, as he puts it, "the phenomenal character we are confronted with" is experienced as a quality or cluster of qualities of something external.[3] In his view, to deny this point is to fail to do justice to the phenomenology.

How can the qualities that confront Jack and Jill when they introspect be *different* qualities of the tomato, given that neither is misperceiving? Obviously, they are not different colors of the tomato. The tomato is red, and neither Jack nor Jill is making any mistake. The solution, according to Shoemaker, is to realize that the relevant phenomenal qualities are relational qualities of the tomato. The tomato is causing Jack to undergo an experience with intrinsic quality Q_1 under normal lighting conditions, and it is causing Jill to undergo an experience with a very different intrinsic quality Q_2 under the same conditions.

So, Jack, in viewing the tomato, is aware of one relational, external quality and Jill is aware of another. But neither is aware of the pertinent quality as relational. That again would distort the phenomenology. Just as the quality of being heavy is not experienced as relational when something feels heavy even though it is relational, so, too, the relevant qualities here are not experienced as relational either. These qualities, Shoemaker says, are "the experienced character of redness" for Jack and Jill. Jack's experience correctly represents the tomato as having one experienced character of redness. Jill's experience correctly represents the tomato as having another.

The picture Shoemaker has, then, is this: Jack and Jill both experience redness, but they experience it indirectly by experiencing another quality. The latter quality is a quality of the tomato, just as redness is, for neither is misperceiving at any level. But the quality is different in the two cases. It is the representation of this quality—the experienced character of redness—that endows Jack's experience with its phenomenal character, and likewise for Jill. Redness has a different experienced character, a different appearance in the two cases, and so the experiences are phenomenally different. Since the experienced character itself brings in an intrinsic quality of experience even though the character is itself a quality of the tomato represented by the experience, Shoemaker is a both a representationalist and an antirepresentationalist: he accepts that phenomenal character is representational but he denies that a full account of phenomenal character can avoid intrinsic qualities of experience.

This is evidently a complex view, complex enough for those of us with a taste for simplicity to be put on our guard. It is also a view that is ultimately unstable. Let me explain.

Consider Jack's experience. The tomato looks red to him. His experience represents it as red. However, on Shoemaker's view, there is a sense in which Jack is not directly aware of the color red in experiencing red. For colorwise, as he views the facing surface of the tomato, he does not directly experience two different qualities covering that surface: red and the experienced character of red. Rather, as noted above, the claim must be that what Jack really immediately experiences is the experienced character of red. Just as Jack sees the tomato indirectly—in the sense that he sees it in virtue of seeing the facing surface of it—so, too, he is aware of red in virtue of being aware of the experienced character of red.

This seems to me counterintuitive. In general, we see things by seeing their facing surfaces, and we see facing surfaces by seeing their color. Intuitively, there is no more basic level of seeing than the seeing of colors—just as there is no more basic level of hearing than the hearing of loudness, pitch, and so forth. Shoemaker is committed to denying this. In his view, since Jack sees the redness of the surface of the tomato by seeing another property not itself a color at all—that of currently causing an experience with a certain intrinsic feature Q_1 (at least according to Shoemaker [1994][4]), colors are not basically seen. They are seen by seeing their experienced character. This claim creates a number of further problems.

To begin with, as Shoemaker himself admits, once we adopt his line on the qualities that are directly experienced in color perception, we must accept that *those* qualities cannot be instantiated by objects at times at which the objects are not seen. That, however, is exceedingly odd. Intuitively, it seems wrongheaded to hold that ripe tomatoes *cannot* have the quality I directly experience them as having in color perception, when no one is looking. Suppose, for example, my direct experience is veridical: the tomato really has the quality I experience as having. Still, in Shoemaker's view, that quality is not possessed (and indeed could not be possessed) by the tomato when no one is seeing it. But intuitively, if my immediate experience is accurate, the quality I directly experience is one that covers the surface of the tomato, even at times at which no one is viewing the tomato.[5]

Another objection to Shoemaker's 1994 proposal is as follows. Suppose that the lighting conditions are very strange and the ripe tomato looks bright purple to me. Suppose also that there are no cases of spectrum inversion. Then intuitively, the tomato does not have the quality it is directly experienced as having. But it does have the quality of currently causing Q, where Q is an intrinsic quality of my present visual experience.

One way to try to handle these objections is to say that the phenomenal character of an experience with intrinsic quality Q is the relational property: having the tendency to cause Q in normal lighting conditions. But in whom is the relevant tendency supposed to be produced? Evidently, it will not do to claim that if the experience is one I am presently undergoing, its phenomenal character is the tendency to cause Q in *me* in normal lighting conditions. For the visual experiences of others (sometimes) have that phenomenal character and would have done so, even if I had never existed.

Shoemaker's latest attempt to spell out a defensible proposal (in his 2000 and amplified in correspondence) consists in holding that phenomenal character is the disposition to produce an experience with a certain intrinsic quality in normal lighting conditions in any creature having a visual system capable of producing experiences with that intrinsic quality. This is certainly unacceptable, however. Consider Jack and Jill again. Jack undergoes an experience with intrinsic quality Q_1, as he views the ripe tomato in good lighting conditions. On the new proposal, the phenomenal character of Jack's visual experience is the disposition to produce Q_1 in normal lighting conditions in any creature having a visual system capable of producing Q_1. Unfortunately, that makes Jack's experience inaccurate. Since the tomato is not disposed to produce Q_1 in Jill in good light even though Jill's visual system is *capable* of producing Q_1 (and it does so when Jill sees grass, for example), the tomato is not disposed to produce Q_1 in normal lighting conditions in any creature having a visual system capable of producing Q_1. So, the tomato does not have the relational property that Jack's visual experience supposedly represents it as having.

A very different sort of objection arises for Shoemaker in connection with his view (to which I earlier urged he is committed in his 1994) that colors are not basically seen. If this is the case, then it is epistemically possible for colors to be absent when the relevant relational properties are present. Compare this with that of seeing a table by seeing a certain facing surface. It is epistemically possible to experience the facing surface, and to do so accurately, even though the whole table is missing (the back having been removed, say). Likewise, if colors are seen by seeing other qualities, not themselves colors, then the fact that a seen object has the qualities it is directly visually experienced as having affords no epistemic guarantee that it has the color the subject of the experience takes it to have or indeed that it has any color it all. That again seems very counterintuitive.

The general problem here is that distinguishing between the experienced character of a color and the color itself effectively draws a veil over the colors. Drawing this veil is tantamount to erecting an appearance/reality distinction for the colors themselves. The coherence of such a distinction is dubious at best, even leaving to one side the above criticism. For how could a *universal*—red, say—appear phenomenally other than it is? A red thing might appear green, but redness could not appear green any more than roundness might appear square. And once the distinction is made, we are locked again in a kind of Cartesian Theatre. Our direct access is just to the qualities on our side of the veil. The rest lies beyond our direct consciousness.

Schoemaker (2000) denies that his theory has this consequence. In response to the above criticism (Tye 2000), he comments:

> To a first approximation, an object's having a phenomenal color property just is its looking a certain way to certain perceivers in virtue of having a certain color, and this normally amounts to the color of the object presenting itself in one of the ways it can present itself. . . . So, it is quite wrong to say . . . that colors "are not basically seen."

I am not persuaded. Consider the phenomenal property Jack directly experiences as covering the surface of the tomato. One can certainly stipulate that that property is a phenomenal *color* property only if it meets the condition Shoemaker specifies in the passage above, in which case one has built into the concept of a phenomenal color property that an object has it in virtue of having a certain color (and hence that it is conceptually impossible for an object to have a given phenomenal color property without having the appropriate color). But now my point restated is that, on Shoemaker's view, it is epistemically (and logically) possible that the phenomenal property Jack experiences as covering the tomato is not a phenomenal *color* property.[6]

There is a further difficulty. Intuitively, in my view, the qualities we directly experience in color perception are experienced by us as nonrelational, as intrinsic to the things we see. But, according to Shoemaker, this is not the case. As noted earlier, our experience of these qualities is really like our experience of weight. We experience the weight of an object without thereby being aware of its relational nature. Likewise for the experienced character of a color. This seems to me to get things backward. In the case of weight, we directly experience something intrinsic, namely mass. We feel the heaviness of a bar of gold by feeling its mass; and mass is not relational. Exactly the opposite is true on Shoemaker's view of color and its experienced character. By seeing a certain experienced character (itself a relational quality though not experienced as such), we see the color of a surface (itself intuitively nonrelational). That seems very strange indeed.

The upshot is that moderation is in trouble. Notwithstanding the complexity of his account, Shoemaker has not succeeded in finding a secure middle ground between the pure representationalist position on phenomenal character and antirepresentationalism, a ground that also respects the phenomenological point to which G. E. Moore first drew our attention in his remark about the sensation of blue.[7] What is motivating Shoemaker, of course, is the desire to make room for the possibility of inverted qualia without adopting a stance that conflicts with Moore on the phenomenology. The question thus arises as to whether that desire can be satisfied by pure representationalism. In the next section, I shall argue that it can.

5.2   Inverted Spectrum Cases

Ned Block (1990, p. 58) remarks: "Spectrum inversion can be understood easily by children. . . . Try it out on the next eight-year-old you encounter. Indeed, they sometimes come up with the idea themselves."

We can certainly agree with Block that it is easy for adults and children alike to grasp the idea of two people (you and I, say) having color experiences that are phenomenally inverted relative to one another. But that, of course, presents no problem for pure representationalism; for you might have an experience of green when I have an experience of red, an experience of yellow when I have an experience of blue, and so on. In short, your color experiences might be representationally inverted relative to mine.

Now suppose, however, that you and I agree in the color discriminations we make. We both call ripe tomatoes 'red', grass 'green', and so forth, and we produce the same nonverbal behavior in sorting tests. Again no immediate problem. The intuition that we might have inverted qualia relative to one another is preserved by pure representationalism so long as it is, in principle, possible for people to have color experiences that generate the same discriminatory responses and yet have radically different representational contents. Given that basic experience is nonconceptual, this is not obviously incoherent. Prima facie, visual experiences might be inverted with respect to their nonconceptual contents while eliciting the same cognitive reactions.[8]

Suppose now it is said that you and I might also be normal perceivers in normal circumstances. The pure representationalist is committed to supposing that if our qualia are inverted then, even though we are both normal, at least one of us is constantly misperceiving–that is, at least one of us has color experiences that are wildly wrong with respect to the colors of things. And that, it may be urged, is impossible.

The worry here cannot be that our verbal and nonverbal color behavior is the same but our experiences differ. That, I am allowing, is not obviously incoherent. The worry is rather that a normal perceiver in standard viewing conditions cannot err dramatically at the level of color experience itself.

But why not?[9] Anyone who thinks that this is a conceptual truth needs to consider various actual cases that are often called "normal misperceptions." Consider, for example, the Muller-Lyer diagram (figure 5.1). There are many such examples of normal sensory illusions.[10] If experience can and does err with respect to length (or orientation or shape), why *cannot* it go wrong in the case of color?

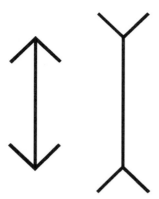

Figure 5.1
The Muller-Lyer diagram.

Some will say that colors are secondary qualities. If something looks red to normal perceivers in standard conditions, then it must be red since redness is a dispositional property of things, defined by reference to a characteristic subjective reaction in normal perceivers in standard conditions. That seems quite implausible, however. For one thing, color irrealism—the thesis that external things are not really colored—is surely a conceptual possibility. Indeed, it may well be the most commonly held view among color scientists (e.g., Cosmides and Tooby, 1995 and Kuehni, 1997).[11] But if color irrealism is conceptually possible, then it is conceptually possible that things are not colored even though they have dispositions to elicit so-called "color experiences" in normal perceivers in standard conditions. This runs counter to the secondary quality analysis. It is also worth noting that by varying the background, the color something appears to have even in standard conditions can be made to vary, just as in the case of length and shape. Indeed, the effect is substantially more pronounced in the case of color. For example, something that appears black in one setting may appear middle gray in another. Likewise, something that appears middle gray can be made to appear white just by changing the background. Contrast effects can be obtained, too, with other colors. View a chocolate bar in sunlight through a tube that is painted matt black on the inside and it will appear yellowy-orange! Look at a blue patch of paint against a red background and it will appear tinged with green.[12]

It seems, then, that normal perceivers in standard conditions not only can but also do undergo color experiences that misrepresent the colors of things. But if this is so, then the pure representationalist can happily allow the possibility of phenomenally inverted color experiences in normal perceivers.[13]

But what if color-qualia inversions are rife? That seems possible; and prima facie, it creates trouble for the pure representationalist. For who now gets to undergo accurate color experiences? Who experiences ripe tomatoes as red, grass as green, and so on? There seems no nonarbitrary way of picking out a subpopulation of normal perceivers whose color experiences do not misrepresent. Any choice of a sub-population seems as good as any other. However, if that is the case, then there is no fact of the matter about who is misrepresenting. So, it seems, there cannot be rife phenomenal inversions on the pure representational view.

A similar difficulty arises in the case of interspecies inversions. Shoemaker has urged that there might be other species of creatures whose color discriminations are as good as ours but who have color experiences that are phenomenally inverted relative to ours. He claims that to say that these creatures are misperceiving color would be wholly implausible. They have as much a right to accurate color experiences as we do. To say that they are wrong and we are right is to make a wholly arbitrary selection. Here, according to Shoemaker, is another inversion scenario that the pure representationalist cannot handle.

Let me begin my reply with the interspecies case. Suppose we grant again that behaviorally undetectable inverted spectra are genuinely possible. Then we should all grant Shoemaker's initial premise: there could indeed be other creatures whose color discriminations match ours even though *phenomenally* their color experiences are reversed. This presents no immediate difficulty for the pure representationalist since, as I have stressed, identity in discriminatory responses does not entail identity in the content of nonconceptual experiences. There could be creatures who behave as we do, even though they are under a series of large-scale community-wide sensory illusions with respect to color.

According to Shoemaker, it is implausible to suppose that such creatures are possible. But why? If there can be normal sensory illusions and ones that are universal in humans, there is surely nothing that rules out the abstract possibility that the normal members of some other species are subject to universal sensory illusions with respect to color.

Granted, these hypothetical creatures have as much a right to accurate color experiences as we do. Without further information, it would certainly be arbitrary to say that we are right and they are wrong at the level of sensory experiences. But so what? Only if no further story *could* coherently be constructed under which they end up being in the wrong while we remain in the right is there any problem here for pure representationalism.

Such a story can be given in teleological terms. Suppose, for example, there is a genetic defect in certain alien creatures that are alive today, the result of which is that wires are crossed in their visual system, thereby inducing in them color experiences opposite to those that were present (in the same conditions) in most of the aliens' ancestors. Originally only a small subpopulation of the aliens had the given defect, but now it has spread so that it is almost universal. Today's aliens have an experience of red when they see green things in daylight; they have an experience of green when they see red things in daylight, and so on. Their experiences are now tracking colors that are opposite on the hue circle to those tracked by their biologically normal ancestors. Since the visual systems of today's aliens are not functioning as they were designed to do, the colors their sensory states *would* track, *were* they discharging their biological function, are not the colors they actually track. Accordingly, given that sensory representation is a matter of causal covariation under optimal conditions,[14] there is species-wide sensory misrepresentation with respect to color.

A story of the same sort can be told in the intraspecies case. Widespread inverted spectra could result by virtue of widespread genetic or biological defects causing the visual system to operate in ways different from those it was originally designed to operate in, thereby inducing misrepresentation.

Alternatively, a story might be developed wherein the external conditions in which the aliens find themselves today are importantly different from those that were present when their visual systems evolved. This external change could itself induce misrepresentation.

Still, it might be insisted, rife intraspecies inverted spectra are possible even where there are no genetic defects. Similarly, undetectable inversions are possible in the interspecies case even when the alien creatures are biologically normal and operating in design conditions. Cases of these sorts lie beyond the resources of the pure representationalist.

This seems to me too hasty. To begin with, the thesis that the sensory representation of color is teleological in character is not itself plausibly viewed as a conceptual truth. Anti-adaptationists claim that some mental (and physical) features of living creatures may not have been selected. Such features in some species may be accidentally produced. This position is, of course, rejected by adaptationists. But it is certainly conceptually possible that anti-adaptationism is true. The dispute here is an empirical one about the actual facts. Those philosophers who endorse a teleological theory of content side with the adaptationists, but they do not deny (or at least should not deny) the conceptual possibility of anti-adaptationism.[15]

Consider next the thesis, apparently held by Brentano (1973) and Meinong (1960), that mental representation generally involves a primitive, unique, nonphysical relation of aboutness, a relation that in some cases (at least according to Meinong) has nonexistent entities among its relata (as, for example, when one thinks about unicorns). I find no conceptual incoherence in this view or any view that takes representation as unique and primitive. Prima facie, it is conceptually possible that such a view is true. Of course, the Brentano/Meinong position is not one that fits with naturalism or physicalism, but that cuts no ice against its *conceptual* coherence.

Given these points, it seems to me that the representationalist can happily allow the *conceptual* possibility of interspecies and rife, intraspecies inverted spectra even where there are no biological or genetic defects. For it is conceptually possible that sensory representation has nothing to do with natural teleology. Indeed, it is conceptually possible that such representation is unique and primitive. As far as our concepts are concerned, it could be the case that God (or some evil genius) decided that the aliens should have their sensory states standardly bear the special and primitive nonphysical relation of aboutness to colors that are not possessed by the objects they are viewing—colors that are inverted relative to those we experience—even though they make the same color discriminations as we do. Similarly, it could be that God, for reasons we cannot comprehend, decided that every third human should have his or her sensory states 'reach out' or be 'about' colors other than those the perceived things have. Indeed, this could be the case even without God. It is conceptually possible, for example, that 50 percent of biologically normal humans, as they view the clear sky, undergo a sensory state that bears the special, primitive relation of aboutness to the color possessed by lemons, while the other 50 percent undergo a sensory state that bears such a relation to blue, the color the sky actually possesses.

So long as these cases are conceptually possible, whatever their metaphysical status, the pure representationalist is on secure ground in allowing the possibility of rife intraspecies inverted spectra even without genetic defects. Surely the fundamental intuition about inverted spectra, whatever the details of individual cases, is that such cases are *coherently thinkable*, that, in reflecting upon the various scenarios, we cannot rule them out on the basis of our reflection alone. Just as we can coherently think that Hesperus is not Phosperus or that water is not H$_2$O, so, too, we can coherently think that sensory misrepresentation is rife among biologically normal humans, even if these things are all metaphysically impossible.

This point is an extremely important one, for it can be brought to bear upon one very extreme case not yet broached: that of rife phenomenal inversions in a population of swamp duplicates of humans (that is, creatures who are molecule-by-molecule duplicates of humans but who are accidentally produced in one way or another and thus lack an evolutionary history). This case seems a very long way from the inversion case accessible to children with which we began. But whatever our views about the metaphysical status of the teleological theory of sensory representation, we need not deny that the above swamp inversion scenario is *conceptually* possible, however bizarre we may find it, *even if* we accept the representational view of qualia. For again all we need to insist is that it is conceptually possible that there is a special, primitive relation of aboutness that connects the sensory states of subpopulations of swamp creatures to different colors in the same everyday perceptual circumstances.

I want to emphasize here that the idea that sensory representation involves a primitive and special, nonphysical relation is not one that need enter into the content of our thoughts with respect to the inversions just mooted. We can conceive of the relevant representational inversions in swamp creatures or in a group of biologically normal humans without thinking of those inversions *as* involving a special relation of the Brentano/Meinong sort. My claim is rather that the conceptual possibility of the Brentano/Meinong view can be appealed to in defense of the position that certain representational inversions are conceptually possible. Once these inversions are allowed, the pure representationalist has no difficulty whatsoever in conceptually allowing the relevant phenomenal inversions. To any advocate of inverted qualia who is inclined to deny that our concepts allow us to think coherently that it is possible for swampmen to undergo certain sensory representational inversions (and hence certain phenomenal inversions, on the pure representational view), I respond that this is conceptually possible since our concepts do not preclude the possibility that subgroups of swampmen undergo sensory states that bear the special Brentano/Meinong relation to different colors in the same standard perceptual circumstances even though they agree in their color discriminations.[16]

Perhaps it will be replied that we can conceive of there being phenomenal inversions among color experiences even while simultaneously conceiving that there is no representational difference between those experiences, whether we are dealing with swamp creatures or human beings. If so, it may be said, the points I have just made are not compelling. To this I reply that pure representationalism should not be taken to have the status of a wholly conceptual or a priori truth. Those of us who think that Moore's point about the transparency of experience is undeniable are committed to holding that the phenomenal character of an experience is not a quality of the experience. That much is indeed a priori, in the broad sense of "a priori" that rules out any appeal to perceptual beliefs or empirical evidence beyond introspection. But the further hypothesis that the representationalist proposes is not a priori. It is (or should be) proposed as offering the best *explanation* of various facts about phenomenal experience. Representationalism is not the only game in town, however, even for those who find Moore's transparency point undeniable. For example, it is surely conceivable that the introspected qualities are really qualities of nonphysical sensa *presented* to us by external things (as Moore himself held in some of his writings). On this view, when I see a tomato, say, what I directly experience are qualities of an immaterial surface or expanse presented to me by the tomato, not qualities of the real tomato (or my visual experience). Therefore, the experienced qualities always have bearers (indeed bearers that exist). What is sometimes absent is a physical object corresponding to the bearer.

The representationalist should concede that such a position is not ruled out a priori by introspection. For the sense-datum theory, like representationalism, denies that the qualities to which we have access when we introspect our experiences are *qualities of the experiences*. What Moore rightfully insisted was that the qualities that individuate our experiences phenomenally are qualities of the *objects* of the experiences. These objects for Moore are special, immaterial entities. Here, of course, the representationalist disagrees. What the representationalist should insist is that representationalism has many advantages over the sense-datum view and no disadvantages. Think, for example, of the metaphysical complexity of the sensum view, the causal difficulties introduced by the postulation of nonphysical sensa, the issue of their necessary privacy, the speckled hen problem, and so on. For these and other reasons, representationalism is to be preferred to the sense-datum theory. The former theory in its pure form, I maintain, gives us the best account of the nature of visual experience and its phenomenal character, *consistent with what introspection tells us*. As such, it has the status of a (partly) a posteriori, metaphysically necessary truth, not a purely a priori, conceptually necessary one. Thus, the pure representationalist can admit with impunity the conceptual possibility of phenomenal inversions without representational difference in both swamp duplicates and human beings.

Finally, what about the *metaphysical* possibility of phenomenal inversions in a population of swamp creatures whose color discriminations are the same as ours? I shall now argue that the representationalist can allow even this possibility without undermining her position. Given transparency, phenomenal inversions occur in the swamp population as long as the color qualities some swamp creatures directly experience are complementary to those others directly experience in the same perceptual circumstances. Assume now that in actual fact, there are very few, if any, phenomenal inversions with respect to color in the *human* population. Then, given transparency, assuming no current population-wide color-vision abnormality (in the teleological sense of "abnormality"), the quality actual humans typically directly experience, viewing blue things, is blue; viewing yellow things, yellow, and so on. It follows that, in the imaginary swamp population, those creatures who directly experience what actual humans typically do as they view blue things, experience the quality of blueness, while those whose experiences are phenomenally inverted directly experience yellow in the presence of blue things. Accordingly, at the nonconceptual, sensory level, some of the swamp creatures have *accurate* experiences, some *inaccurate*.[17] For some of the swamp creatures, things are as they appear phenomenally, but not so for others.[18] Blue things look (phenomenally) blue to some of them— to those swamp creatures who directly experience the quality we typically directly experience in seeing those things—but blue things look (phenomenally) yellow to others—to those swamp creatures who, in the presence of blue things, directly experience the quality we typically directly experience in seeing yellow things. There is no difficulty, then, for the representationalist in allowing the metaphysical possibility of phenomenal inversions in a group of swamp creatures. Since representational inversions within the group are metaphysically possible, phenomenal inversions are too.[19]

The conclusion I draw is that even if Shoemaker is right in supposing that commonsense allows the possibility of inverted spectra, pure representationalism is not seriously threatened. When confronted with various inversion scenarios, the representionalist need not draw in his horns in the manner of Shoemaker and opt for a hybrid or mixed view of phenomenal character. This, I suggest, is all to the good since the mixed view is much more complex than the pure one, and moderation of the sort Shoemaker proposes does not work anyway.

Notes

1. See, e.g., Block (1990, 1996).

2. See Shoemaker (1994). In a reply to some of the criticisms I offer below of his position, Shoemaker (2000) maintains that although he has appealed to inverted spectra to motivate his view in earlier work, actual differences between normal color perceivers themselves necessitate an account of the sort he offers. For example, according to Shoemaker, I may see something as unique blue while you see it as a slightly greenish blue without either one of us misperceiving. He also comments: "Nothing in the reflectances, or in the light . . . corresponds to the difference between unique and nonunique hues." For a reply to the former point, see the section "Sexism, Racism, and Ageism" in chapter 4. For a reply to the latter, see chapter 7.

3. See Shoemaker, 1996.

4. This proposal is preferred by Shoemaker to several others canvassed in his 1994. In Shoemaker 1996 and Shoemaker 2000, slightly different proposal are made. Shoemaker claims (in his 2000) that is a mistake to attribute to him the view that colors are not basically seen. For more, see below, this section.

5. This objection also undercuts the slightly different proposal that, for each color experience, its phenomenal character is a relational property of the type: *causing an experience with such-and-such an intrinsic quality in normal lighting conditions.*

6. One might reply that this objection collapses if colors are given a secondary quality analysis. However, such an analysis is incompatible with Shoemaker's position on inverted spectra (which position motivates his approach to the phenomenology of color experience in the first place). As Shoemaker himself acknowledges, on his view, "the association of particular phenomenal properties with particular colors is contingent" (Shoemaker 2000).

7. See chapter 3, p. 47 and the surrounding discussion.

8. Here I oversimplify. On my account of phenomenal concepts, experiences that are inverted with respect to their nonconceptual contents will elicit different *purely phenomenal* judgments. These judgments, however, will themselves play the same functional roles with respect to nonphenomenal color judgments and behavior. The phenomenally inverted experiences will therefore produce the same pattern of discriminatory responses notwithstanding their different contents. Or so at least I am prepared to grant for present purposes. For some reservations, see Tye (1995, chapter 7). These reservations neither stem from the thesis of representationalism nor do they threaten that thesis. Rather, they lead me to wonder whether full-blooded color inversion scenarios are really conceptually possible, after all. In this chapter, I am going to put such reservations to one side.

9. Perhaps it will be said that in raising this question, I am being inconsistent. For did I not earlier criticize Shoemaker for taking a position that allows that things might not have the colors normal perceivers take them to have in stan-

dard conditions? No, I did not. I criticized Shoemaker for holding a view that allows the possibility of things not having the colors normal perceivers take them to have in standard conditions *even though they do have the qualities they are directly experienced as having.*

10. For other cases, see chapter 7.

11. Some philosophers also hold this view, e.g., Boghossian and Velleman (1989).

12. For more on contrast effects, see chapter 7.

13. Here and above, I am supposing a normal perceiver is one who passes the appropriate, standard color-discrimination tests. I do not mean a biologically normal perceiver.

14. For more on the causal-covariation view and how the notion of optimal conditions is best understood, see chapter 6.

15. Adopting the teleological story for sensory representation certainly does not commit one to supposing that wherever *any* color differences occur between two individuals, at least one of them is misrepresenting. For some relevant comments on individual color differences, see chapter 4, case 7 and chapter 7, note 23.

16. Again I leave to one side the reservations mentioned in note 8, above.

17. In the phenomenal sense of the term 'looks', the clear sky looks yellow to the swamp creatures with inaccurate experiences. But it certainly looks *like* other blue things to them. So, in the comparative sense of the term 'looks', it looks blue. For more on comparative appearing and how it differs from phenomenal appearing, see chapter 3. I might add that, on my view of phenomenal concepts, those swamp creatures with phenomenally inaccurate experiences do not misapply their phenomenal color concepts to those experiences. For example, they judge correctly that the clear sky looks yellow to them, in the purely phenomenal sense of the terms 'looks'. Likewise, they apply correctly their nonphenomenal color concepts (concepts of a sort they share with Frank Jackson's Mary while she is imprisoned, or a man born blind who never regains his sight) in beliefs/judgments as to the colors of things they see (in typical cases). For example, they believe that the clear sky is blue. Mistakes arise in certain cognitive contexts, however. For example, the swamp creatures mistakenly believe that the color quality of which they are directly aware whenever they view the clear sky—the quality they conceive of under the phenomenal concept *yellow* via introspection of their visual experiences of the clear sky—is blue (in the nonphenomenal sense of the term 'blue').

18. Given that the external environment is the same for all the swamp creatures, the fact that some of them are *mis*representing is a reflection of the operation of their color visual systems. Those systems for some of the creatures are not *optimal*. The processing that is going on in some of the swamp creatures is *interfering* with the production of accurate color experiences. This fits straightforwardly with the model of sensory representation I endorse, namely, that of

tracking or causal covariation in optimal conditions. For more on this, see chapter 6, section 6.3.

19. Suppose that in actual fact, rife color inversions occur within the human population. In this case, there is still no difficulty. Now, at the nonconceptual, sensory level, only some human experiences are accurate. For others, genetic abnormalities interfere with the production of veridical color experiences in standard conditions. Those swamp creatures who experience, in the presence of blue objects, the same quality as those humans with no pertinent genetic abnormalities, have accurate experiences. The remaining swamp creatures, at the phenomenal level—and *only* at that level—are deluded. The argument now goes as in the text.

6

Swampman Meets Inverted Earth

Ned Block has argued forcefully in several places (e.g., 1990, 1996) that the example of Inverted Earth refutes the externalist variety of representationalism. Another well-known problem case for externalist representationalism is that of Swampman. These two examples, it can be argued, work together in such a way as to impale the representationalist[1] on the horns of a dilemma. In this chapter, I want to show that there is a way out of this dilemma. Nothwithstanding initial appearances, a safe path exists for the representationalist between the Scylla of Inverted Earth and the Charybdis of Swampman.

The chapter is divided into four sections. Section 6.1 poses the dilemma. Sections 6.2 and 6.3 discuss what might be called the "hardline" response. It is argued that this response, even though it can handle many of the objections that have been raised to it, is ultimately unsatisfactory. Section 6.4 defends an alternative, more natural, and softer reply that is available to the representationalist.

6.1 The Problem

Inverted Earth is an imaginary planet on which things have complementary colors to the colors of their counterparts on Earth. The sky is yellow, grass is red, ripe tomatoes are green, and so on. The inhabitants of Inverted Earth undergo psychological attitudes and experiences with inverted intentional contents relative to those of people on Earth. They think that the sky is yellow, see that grass is red, and so forth. However, they call the sky 'blue', grass 'green', ripe tomatoes 'red', just as we do. Indeed, in all respects consistent with the alterations just described, Inverted Earth is as much like Earth as possible.

In Block's original version of the tale, one night while you are asleep, a team of alien scientists insert color-inverting lenses in your eyes and take you to Inverted Earth, where you are substituted for your Inverted Earth twin or *doppelgänger*. Upon awakening, you are aware of no difference, since the inverting lenses neutralize the inverted colors.[2] You think that you are still where you were before. What it is like for you when you see the sky or anything else is just what it was like on Earth. But after enough time has passed, after you have become sufficiently embedded in the language and physical environment of Inverted Earth, your intentional contents will come to match those of the other inhabitants. You will come to believe that the sky is yellow, for example, just as they do. Similarly, you will come to have a visual experience that represents the sky as yellow because the experiential state you now undergo, as you view the sky, is the one that, in you, now normally tracks yellow things. So, the later you will come to be subject to inner states that are intentionally inverted relative to the inner states of the earlier you, while the phenomenal aspects of your experiences will remain unchanged. It follows that strong representationalism of the externalist sort is false.[3]

In Block's latest version of the Inverted Earth story (1996), you are not kidnapped by alien scientists. Instead, you are aware of traveling to the new planet, and once you are there, you make a conscious decision to adopt the concepts of the locals. According to Block, this alteration has two advantages:

> ... First, it makes it clearer that you become a member of the new community. On the old version, one might wonder what you would say if you found out about the change. Perhaps you would insist on your membership in the old community and defer to it rather than the new one. The new version also makes it easier to deal with issues of remembering your past of the sort brought up in connection with the inverted spectrum in Dennett, 1991. (Block 1996, p. 42)

One simple reply that the strong representationalist can make with respect to this objection is to deny that there really is any change in normal tracking with respect to color, at least as far as your experiences go. "Normal," after all, has both teleological and nonteleological senses. If what an experience normally tracks is what nature designed it to track, what it has as its biological purpose to track, then shifting environments from Earth to Inverted Earth will make no difference to normal tracking and hence no difference to the representational contents of your experiences. The sensory state that nature designed in your species to track blue in the setting in which your species evolved will continue to do just that even if through time, on Inverted Earth, in that alien environment, it is usually caused in you by looking at yellow things.

The suggestion that tracking is telological in character, at least for the case of basic experiences, goes naturally with the view that states like feeling pain or having a visual sensation of red are phylogenetically fixed. On this view, through learning, we can change our beliefs, our thoughts, our judgments, but not our basic sensory experiences.

This reply to the Inverted Earth objection, tempting though it is, faces a formidable difficulty. It entails that accidental replicas of actual sentient creatures lack all experiences. Consider, for example, the case of the swamp creature formed by the chemical reaction that takes place in a swamp after a lightning bolt hits a log there. Swampman, as he is usually known, is an accidental molecule-by-molecule duplicate of some actual human being, but he has no evolutionary history. On a cladistic conception of species, Swampman is not human. Indeed, lacking any evolutionary history, he belongs to no species at all. His inner states play no teleological role. Nature did not design any of them to do anything. So, if phenomenal character is a certain sort of teleo-representational content, then Swampman has no experiences.

One brave representationalist, Fred Dretske, embraces this conclusion (Dretske, 1995). However, his response is not, I think, a promising one. For one thing, it is highly counterintuitive. For another, Dretske could conceivably find out that he himself is a swamp creature. If this were to occur, then, as a strong representationalist, it appears that he would be committed to supposing that he had never had any experiences. And patently that is as ridiculous for Dretske as it would be for you or me.[4]

Dretske's position has other potential problems. For Dretske, sensory states are hard-wired. Cases in which sensations seem to change with learning are treated as cases of adaptation in beliefs. In Dretske's view, then, swamp creatures cannot acquire any sensory states through learning. However, swamp creatures, through time, certainly can come to have new beliefs. For example, given suitable training, Swampchild can come to learn to recognize dogs on sight, and in so doing she acquires the concept *dog*. Suppose that with more sophisticated training, Swampchild comes to grasp that in abnormal lighting, things are not always as they appear. By using her eyes, she comes to recognize when things appear square, for example, and she distinguishes that from being square. Then Swampchild ends up hopelessly deluded. She believes that the coin appears round to her, that the television screen appears rectangular, just as I do, but, unlike me, she is completely wrong throughout her life. In reality, nothing ever appears any way to her at all. Radical error of this sort seems inconceivable in my own case. How, then, can it be allowed for Swampchild, given that conceivably *I* originated in the swamp?

One way for Dretske to try to handle this objection is to argue that Swampchild could *not* acquire any concepts pertaining to how things appear, no matter what course of training she undertook. The obvious and immediate difficulty with this strategy is that it entails that, in my own case, if I was once a swampchild, I do not have any conception of the appearance/reality distinction, indeed that I do not understand the objection I am now raising. But that surely, again, cannot be right. The conclusion to which we seem to be led is that either strong representationalism is false or a nonteological notion of normal tracking is needed to underwrite the appeal to externalist representational content. Let us, then, consider nonteleological tracking.

What a state normally tracks can be understood to be what it usually tracks after a sufficiently deep embedding in a given socioenvironmental setting. If, for example, I move to a new community and through time come to defer to experts in the community with respect to whether items fall within the extensions of terms I use, then, according to many externalists, the concepts I express by those terms will come to mirror those of others in the community. Likewise, the experiences I undergo will change their contents as they come to be causally correlated, in the new setting, with different worldly items and to give rise to behavior appropriate to them. Given this notion of normal tracking, if I move to Inverted Earth and I participate fully in the community, my visual experiences, as I look at the sky and other yellow things, will come to represent them as yellow.

The difficulty strong representationalism now faces is, of course, that the phenomenal character of my visual experiences remains the same with the move to Inverted Earth. Here is what Block says:

> Imagine that on the birthday just before you leave for Inverted Earth you are looking at a clear blue sky. Your visual experience represents it as blue. Years later, you have a birthday party on Inverted Earth and you look at the Inverted Earth sky. Your visual experience represents it as yellow. . . . But the phenomenal character remains the same, as indicated by the fact that you can't tell the difference. So, there is a gap between the representational content of experience and its phenomenal character. (1996, p. 43)

Once again, then, it appears that representationalism is false.

It might now be suggested that what the representationalist needs is a "mixed" theory of tracking in normal or optimal conditions. For creatures or devices with states that were designed to track things, for example, human beings and thermometers, those states acquire representational content at least partly via what they track under design conditions. Here, if design conditions fail to obtain, then the setting is abnormal, no matter how long it obtains. For a speedometer used in a car with tires of the wrong size—tires other than those it was designed to be used with—the position of the pointer *mis*represents the speed of the car, even if the speedometer is never hooked up to tires of the right size.

For accidental replicas (for example, Swampman) the requirements are different. Swampman, although he is not human, is self-sustaining, energy-using, capable of reproduction. By any reasonable standard, he is alive, even in the absence of an evolutionary history. Moreover, there are conditions under which he will flourish, and there are conditions under which he will not. If objects in the external environment trigger internal states in Swampman that elicit behavior inappropriate to those objects—if, say, light rays bend in peculiar ways, thereby causing Swampman to misidentify very badly the shapes and sizes of things—then he isn't going to last long. His needs won't be met; he won't easily survive the predations of others.

This leads to the thought that Swampman can have inner states that acquire representational content via the tracking or causal covariation that takes place under conditions of *well functioning*. However this is further spelled out—whether or not, for example, it is demanded that he become a full-fledged member of some appropriate community—the general suggestion is that, where the representational contents of experiences are concerned, what counts as tracking in normal conditions can vary with the kind of creature or system we are dealing with. Where there is a design, normal conditions are those in which the creature or system was designed to operate. Where there is no design, normal conditions are, more broadly, those in which the creature or system happens to be located or settled, if it is functioning well (for a sufficient period of time) in that environment.

This may initially seem to provide the representationalist with a route between the Swampman problem and the Inverted Earth example. Swamp duplicates may now be credited with experiences, according to the representationalist theory; moreover, if you or I travel to Inverted Earth, the representational contents of our experiences remain the same in the corresponding situations. Unfortunately, the path leads to a dead end, for if we can travel from Earth to Inverted Earth, so, too, can swamp creatures. The case of the traveling swampman, equipped with inverting lenses, lies beyond the resources of the above mixed, representational theory. Here, representational content will change, but phenomenal character will remain the same. Representationalism, it seems, is in deep trouble.

In summary, then, the dilemma for the externalist representationalist is as follows. Either normal tracking is teleological or it is not. If it is, then Inverted Earth is no problem but Swampman is. If normal tracking is not telelogical, then Swampman can be handled but not Inverted Earth. To try to pass between the horns of the dilemma by holding that normal tracking is sometimes teleological and sometimes not is to be stopped dead in one's tracks by the hybrid case of the Swampman who travels to Inverted Earth.

6.2   Biting the Bullet on the Inverted Earth Objection:
A Reply to Block

In this section, I want to lay out and discuss a possible hard-line response that the representationalist might make. I shall begin by returning again to the initial Inverted Earth case and, *for present purposes*, I shall grant Block's assertion that with the move to Inverted Earth, representational content changes. Block claims that even with the switch in representational content, phenomenal character remains the same. Now it is certainly true that if I make the trip (and I am an ordinary, philosophically unsophisticated speaker without any knowledge of a change in my environment), I am going to *say* (and believe) that the looks of things have not altered. But, of course, I am relying here, in part, on my memory of the past looks of things. Block assumes that such memories can be trusted. Is he right?

Consider first the following example in which memory goes wrong. I am kidnaped and taken to Putnam's famous planet, Twin Earth, on which there is no water, but instead 'twater', a liquid that is superficially just like water. After I have spent sufficient time on Twin Earth, many externalists would say that the concept I express by 'water' shifts. In uttering "Water is wet," what I come to mean is that twater is wet, just like everyone else on Twin Earth. Suppose now I say, "I take my gin with water just as I did in my undergraduate years." My word 'water' now means twater; so, the belief I express here is false (assuming I switched to Twin Earth after getting my B.A.). As an undergraduate, I drank water, not twater. The "memory" on which my belief is based is really a mis-memory, induced by the deep shift in my external relations: I am no longer referring to the same liquid by the word 'water' as I did in my youth.

Perhaps the reply will be that this just *assumes* externalism for memory contents.[5] Some argument is needed. Let us begin with the following case: I am on Earth, holding a flagon of water in my hand. I sincerely utter the sentence, "I drank two pints of water from a flagon yesterday without pausing." My molecular twin, on Twin Earth, utters the very same sentence. He has never left Twin Earth, just as I have never left Earth. Neither of us has engaged in any fanciful space travel to bizarre alternative planets. So, he has never seen or tasted or causally interacted with any samples of water, just as I have never done any of these things with respect to twater. In these perfectly mundane circumstances, my twin surely has as much right to be credited with an accurate memory as I do. It cannot be correct to say (in English), then, that his memory is veridical if and only if he drank two pints of *water* yesterday from a flagon without stopping. Rather the accuracy conditions for his memory must advert to *twater*. It follows that memory contents can differ in microphysical duplicates. External factors are relevant to the individuation of memory contents.

In the example just given, my past environment is the same as my present one, and likewise for my twin. What it shows directly is that *past* external factors—those that obtained at the time that the memory representation was laid down—are relevant to the individuation of memory contents expressible in that-clauses that utilize natural kind terms. The example does not yet show that present external factors can override past ones.[6] So, it can still be held that where present and past environments came apart (through traveling), what determines natural kind memory contents is the past environment.

Even so, the above claim is not one that would be universally accepted. The thesis that microphysical duplicates can differ with respect to the contents of their memories, as I am understanding it, is not like the thesis that microphysical duplicates can differ with respect to what they see—at least if the term 'see' is taken to be a success verb. Given that one cannot see X, unless X exists, it trivially follows that one's seeing X does not supervene upon purely internal factors. In the case of the term 'memory', however, at least as I am using the term, having a memory that *p* does not entail that *p*. It could be the case, for example, that I did not drink two pints of water yesterday without pausing—that my memory is inaccurate. Likewise for my twin and his twater memory. Still, the contents of our mistaken memories ('mismemories', if you like) are individuated, in part, by external factors. And that is a substantive externalist thesis.

But what if past and present environments come apart? Which external factors determine content then? Consider next the case in which I sincerely say to you, "Water is the only thing I now drink before 5PM.

Many years ago, however, I drank water fortified by gin in the afternoons. I enjoyed those afternoons; water is improved by mixing it with gin." Suppose that, unknown to me, I am now on Twin Earth, and that I have been for some time. My word 'water', as it is used in the first sentence of my report, means twater (by the usual nonmemory-involving Twin reasoning). In the second sentence, 'water' again means twater. Intuitively, I am still exercising the same concept when I use the word 'water', and in so doing I am making a *comparison* between the present and the past. What I am saying, indeed what I believe if I am sincere, is that twater is the only thing I now drink before 5PM, even though many years ago, I drank twater fortified by gin in the afternoons. In the third sentence, I explain why I enjoyed those distant afternoons by adding that twater is improved by mixing it with gin. This would make no sense if what I really believed is that I drank *water* with gin during those afternoons. My remarks, it seems, are based upon an inaccurate memory. Many years ago on Earth, before I switched to Twin Earth, I drank water, not twater, before 5PM.

The conclusion to which we seem drawn is that where past and present environments come apart, natural kind concepts entering into the contents of propositional memories get their extensions determined by the present environment. This is a strong externalist thesis about memory. It implies, for example, that memories are not always laid down with their contents fixed and then later retrieved. Instead, their contents can float free of the settings that gave rise to them and change with suitable changes in the external setting.

It might be replied that the above example does not adequately support this conclusion. Suppose I am informed that I am now living on Twin Earth, and that I have been for some years. Suppose also I believe my informant. Would I not now correct my previous remarks by saying that I had mis-spoken and that I really believed that I had drunk (Earth) water in my youth? Would I not claim that what I had *wanted* to say was that many years ago I had drunk (Earth) water with gin in the afternoons?

Certainly, I wanted to tell the truth. And now knowing the real facts, I realize that I did not drink twater in my youth. But until a few moments ago, I firmly believed that I had never switched planets. At the time I made my remarks, I also believed that I was on Twin Earth (for I used the term 'Earth' to refer to the same planet as everyone else in my linguistic community). So, I certainly believed that twater was what I used to drink just as it is now. Given the new information, then, my beliefs about the past *change*; I no longer believe what I did. So, I wouldn't *now* say what I did. However, at the time I said what I believed.

Perhaps it will be granted that I believe that twater was not the only thing I used to drink before 5PM. And perhaps it will also be granted that I *take* myself to have a twater memory (i.e., a memory that involves the concept *twater*). Still, it might be said, intuitively, what I really remember is that I used to drink water with gin before 5PM. My belief that I have a twater memory is in error. On this view, externalism is true for the contents of certain beliefs about the past just as it is for the contents of certain beliefs about the present; but it is not true (in any strong sense) for memory contents.

The obvious objection to this reply is that if externalism holds for some beliefs about the past, then it can hardly fail for some thoughts about the past. After all, the normal supposition is that, in believing that *p*, one assents to the very content one entertains in thinking that *p*. Moreover, it is a simple matter to modify the above thought experiment so that it applies directly to thought rather than to belief.[7] But if externalism is true for any thought contents pertaining to the past, then it must surely also be true for the corresponding memory contents (and, in particular, for the memory content that I drank twater with gin before 5PM) since, intuitively, it is part and parcel of remembering that *p* that one think that *p*.[8]

A third objection is that while I do indeed believe that I used to drink twater with gin, it is also true that I believe that I used to drink water with gin. Once the slow switch has been completed, I am subject to both beliefs. My mistake is to suppose that water is the same as twater.

That, however, is very implausible for at least two reasons. For one thing, after many years on Twin Earth I surely am not prepared to apply both the concept *twater* and the concept *water* to the liquid that comes out of taps, fills lakes, and so forth, in my current environment. (I certainly don't believe that, in this case, there is water around here.) For another, if on Twin Earth, I perform a Putnam thought experiment in reverse with respect to Earth, I would surely deny that there is any twater on that planet while simultanously granting that water is found there. How could I do that if I believed that water is twater?

A final objection I shall mention here[9] is that the proposed position simply does not do justice to the strong intuition that there are past episodes I have not forgotten in the described case since I surely retain some memory impressions or images of myself drinking *water* and gin in past afternoons. This last claim seems to me correct as far as it goes. But it concerns memory impressions or images of water rather than propositional memories into which the concept *water* enters. Therefore, it does not undermine the conclusion I have tried to establish thus far, namely that anyone who is moved by Putnam's Twin Earth thought experiments to embrace externalism with respect to certain thought contents pertaining to the present (specifically, those expressible in that-clauses into which natural kind terms enter) should hold a parallel externalist position with respect to the corresponding memory contents.[10]

Returning now to the case of Inverted Earth, the strong representationalist can say that my report of no change in phenomenal character is like the case above in which I make a report of a distant past episode on Earth after having spent many years on Twin Earth: it is necessarily in error. By hypothesis, on the representationalist view, color experiences change their phenomenal character with a change in represented color. When I now say, after a long time on Inverted Earth, "Grass looks green to me now, just as it did five, ten, and twenty years ago," I am wrong. 'Green' (in Inverted English) means red; and grass did not look red to me twenty years ago. My memory has led me astray.

This reply seems an obvious one for the externalist to make, given the hypothesis of a switch in representational content. But Block finds it unsatisfactory. He replies:

The Inverted Earth argument challenges externalist representation[al]ism about phenomenal character, so trotting in externalist representation[al]ism about memory of phenomenal character to defend it seems a bit pathetic. The idea of the Inverted Earth argument is to exploit the first person judgement that in the example as framed the subject *notices no difference*. The subject's experience and memories of that experience reveal no sign of change in environment. . . . The defender of the view that memory is defective must blunt or evade the intuitive appeal of the first person point of view to be successful. It is no good to simply invoke the doctrine that experience is entirely representational. But the reply to the Inverted Earth argument [we are considering] does just that. It says that the memories of the representational contents are wrong, so the memories are wrong too. But that is just to *assume* that as far as memory goes, phenomenal character is representational content. For the argument to have any force, there would need to be some independent reason for taking externalism about phenomenal memory seriously. (1996, pp. 44–5)

This response seems to me very strange. We do, it seems, have first-person authority with respect to a range of mental states. For example, we can, it seems, know what we are thinking in a way different from the way we can know what others are thinking: we can know in a direct and authoritative way what we are thinking; we normally have a kind of "privileged access" to our thoughts. Likewise, we normally have a kind of privileged access with respect to the phenomenal character of our experiences. But privileged access pertains to our *present* mental states. It is not a thesis that pertains to past mental states.

That there are possible situations in which we fail to know our past mental states is clearly illustrated by Twin Earth traveling cases. For example, on Twin Earth, after many years there, I might sincerely say to you, "When I was much younger, I used to think that drinking ten glasses of water would keep the doctor away." Here I believe that I used to have a certain twater thought. But, on Earth, in my youth, I did not have any twater thoughts at all.

One need not resort to such an exotic case to make the point. Everyday examples suffice, examples that are independent of the truth of externalism. One might, say, recall a certain linguistic image one had some years ago, but misremember its content. It is generally agreed that the meanings of one's words can change over a long period of time without one *noticing* any change. One might recall a linguistic auditory image one had in the past and yet misremember its content or meaning, due to a change in the meanings of one's words. Suppose that as a child one used the word *bank* to mean only the bank of a river. As an adult, one also uses the word in its other familiar sense. One might recall an auditory linguistic image one had as a child that involves the sentence "I am going to the bank," and misremember its content, believing that one was thinking that one was going to a bank, in the financial institution sense of the word.[11]

What, then, can be the force of observing that the subject of the move to Inverted Earth notices no difference between his present experiences when he looks at the sky and those he had many years ago? The first person judgment that phenomenally nothing has changed requires a comparison between the present and the past. And privileged access fails for past mental states, whatever their type. We do not know in a direct and authoritative way what *used* to be going on in our minds. So, the "intuitive appeal" of the first person point of view needs no blunting or evading by the representationalist. Moreover, if externalism (of the relevant sort) about content is true, and phenomenal character is representational content, then the first person comparative judgment, in this case, *must* be mistaken. The subject cannot help but misremember his earlier experiences.

Block claims that this last response begs the question. But this is to forget who is giving an argument for what. Block is arguing that representationalism fails since it cannot handle the Inverted Earth example. This example assumes that things now look phenomenally just as they used to look. The representationalist is entitled to question this assumption. Why believe it? What reason can be given for supposing that it is true? I have suggested that the appeal to first person authority that Block makes should not persuade anyone. I have also suggested that independent reasons can be given for being an externalist with respect to propositional memory contents, reasons comparable to those for being an externalist with respect to thought. So, if the report that things look now as they used to look is based upon propositional memory of their looks, then there is strong reason to doubt its veracity.

At this stage, another suggestion might be that even if externalism is defensible with respect to propositional memories, it is not a plausible position with respect to memories of the sort that parallel experience. The latter are what might be called "phenomenal memory images." In the most basic case, they represent to us, in phenomenal form, the past colors, tastes, smells, and so forth we have encountered (or take ourselves to have encountered). Arguably, the claim that the clear sky now looks phenomenally just as it used to do is best viewed as resting, in part, on a phenomenal memory image. It is the comparison of this image of the color of the clear sky on some distant occasion with the present experience, looking skywards, that underwrites the belief that phenomenally the look of the clear sky has not changed. There is no reason to question the accuracy of images of this sort when traveling has occurred.

I concede that this would be the case, if memory images represent in the manner of clear photographs. Then, phenomenal memory image contents would be frozen in time, fixed by the contents of the original perceptual representations that gave rise to them. Traveling could make no difference.

Unfortunately, the photographic model of memory images is incompatible with what we know about how such imagery actually works. For example, it has been found that when people are asked questions about famous faces—whether, for example, Clark Gable or George C. Scott has bushier eyebrows—those who reported having the most vivid memory images tend to be the least accurate.[12] This makes perfectly good sense if generating a memory image is a process that is influenced by concepts, something like producing a sketch or a drawing; for if the instructions in memory that govern the production of the drawing are partial or incomplete, subjects who have vivid images must fill in the gaps themselves at the time of recall without recourse to stored representations of the missing facial features of the relevant people.[13] But if generating a memory image is a matter of retrieving a stored photograph, it is very hard to see what could account for the relative inaccuracy of the vivid imagers.[14]

Perhaps it will now be said that even if the photographic model of images is mistaken, still there is no special reason to question the accuracy of my phenomenal memory images after the switch to Inverted Earth. For intuitively when, on Inverted Earth, I remember the clear sky of my youth, my phenomenal memory image is *of* the blue earthly sky and not *of* the yellow Inverted Earth sky. To see this, consider the following example.[15] One day I see Margaret Thatcher in a bikini on a beach in Spain. Not surprisingly, I find the event memorable and I often speak about it. Later, I am surreptitiously switched with my twin on Twin Earth. To me, things in my new setting are as they always were. Later still, I am introduced to Thatcher's twin, and I refer to her with the name 'Margaret Thatcher'. I get to know her well and I am caused to reminisce about when I first saw her (or rather when I first believe I saw her). I call up a vivid and accurate image. Intuitively, my memory image is *of* the earthly Thatcher, and not of the person I now call 'Thatcher', even though I now *believe* that it is of the latter. So, my switch to Twin Earth does not switch which real individual my memory image is of.

Likewise, I suggest, the representationalist should grant that there is an ordinary sense of 'of' in which my later phenomenal memory image is of the clear blue earthly sky. But it does not follow from this that my phenomenal memory image is accurate. For the fact that the image is of the blue sky (in the relevant sense of 'of') is compatible with supposing that the color it represents the sky as having is yellow. There is no inconsistency here, since the case may be taken to be one of misrepresentation (just as when I am really seeing a straight stick, but I visually represent it as bent).

Still, is there any good *reason* to suppose that there is misrepresentation in this case? It seems to me that there is. I have already argued that I believe that the clear sky looked yellow in the past just as I believe that the clear sky looks yellow now. The former belief, I am now granting, is based upon a phenomenal memory image; the latter upon my visual experience as I view the sky. But if my phenomenal memory image represents the clear Earth sky as *blue* while my present visual experience represents the sky as *yellow*, then how can I believe both that the sky looked yellow in the past and that it looks yellow now? The question I am raising concerns the asymmetry that arises here. How can I cognitively classify the color my phenomenal memory image represents the sky as having (namely, blue, if my image is accurate) as yellow while simultaneously classifying *another* color (namely, yellow—the color my matching visual experience represents the sky as having) as yellow also? The answer surely is that I cannot. On any reasonable account of privileged access, I must be having an inaccurate phenomenal memory image.[16] Both my phenomenal memory image and my present visual experience must represent the clear sky as yellow. It is this identity in content, according to the representationalist, that is responsible for an identity in phenomenal character between the two states.

How phenomenal memory images represent, given their inaccuracy in the appropriate traveling cases, is an interesting question. I have already suggested that they are, in certain respects, more like drawings than photographs. More specifically, I hold that they have a fundamentally matrix-like structure, the cells of which are filled with symbols for such simple perceptible features as color. This is in keeping with what I believe is the most plausible view of image representation generally and fits also with what seem to me the most promising accounts of the format of perceptual experiences.[17] On an account of this sort, if the constituent symbols for color and other such qualities in phenomenal images change their meanings, then the contents of those images shift and diverge from their perceptual sources. The nonteleological externalist claims that such changes occur here just as they do in the cases of propositional memory and thought. More importantly for present purposes, to assert that these symbols in phenomenal memory images do *not* change their meanings with suitable environmental changes is to take a position for which reasons are necessary if such a position is to form part of a persuasive argument against representationalism. And no such reasons are given by Block. On the contrary, he insists that the representationalist, in making phenomenal memory sensitive to external factors, is begging the question. That seems to me very far from being the case, given what I have argued so far.

Nonetheless, Block presses on with the charge that the representationalist is begging the question. He says:

We could dramatize what is question-begging about the argument by augmenting the thought experiment so that the subject understands the philosophical theories that dictate that his representational contents shift. Then, being careful, he will acknowledge that the thought he *used* to think with the words "The sky is blue" is not the same as the thought he now thinks with those words. And he will acknowledge something similar about the representational content of his perception of the sky. So, in the new version of the thought experiment he knows that the representational contents of his experiences have shifted. But that gives him no reason to back down from his insistence that there is no difference in the way the sky looked to him (in one sense of that phrase), that if he could have both experiences to juxtapose, he would not be able to discern a difference. Plainly, he is justified in saying that there is no difference in *something*, something we could call the phenomenal character of the experience of seeing the sky (1996, p. 45).[18]

This again is unpersuasive. Suppose that I am the subject described in the above quote and that I am now on Inverted Earth. Suppose also that in this case I am fully aware of where I am. It is correct to say of me in English that looking at the clear sky today, I know that my visual experience represents yellow. Of course, I would express this knowledge in Inverted English by using the word 'blue', but still the experience represents yellow. I also know that at some earlier time, *t*, when I was on Earth, my visual experience at *t*, looking at the clear sky, represented blue. Reflecting upon these pieces of knowledge, I know that my visual experience today is representationally different with respect to color from my visual experience at *t*.

Reflecting further, am I going to insist that there is no phenomenal difference between my present visual experience and my earlier one? That I will respond in this way is surely no longer obvious. Indeed, if the 'I' of the thought experiment is myself, then the answer is "Certainly not." Since, in my view, the phenomenal character of any phenomenal state (including memory images) is a matter of representational content, it immediately follows that there is a difference between the phenomenal character that is presently accessible to me, via introspection, and the original phenomenal character of my visual experience at *t* (given the representational change).[19] On this account, although my present visual experience phenomenally matches my memory image, it phenomenally differs from the earlier experience. Here there is ample reason to question my memory image and to back down from an "insistence" that phenomenally nothing has changed.

In the latest imagined scenario, then, it is not in the least evident that I will say that something (relevant) in my experience has remained constant, as Block supposes. That is what I *actually* say, reflecting upon my earlier experiences of the sky on clear days. But the counterfactual situation described above is very different from the actual one. In that highly abnormal situation, what I am entitled to claim is only that *phenomenally my memory of the sky matches my present visual experience*. Plainly, I am justified in saying that there is no difference at this phenomenal level. That, however, is not enough for Block's purposes. He also needs to assume that things here are historically just as they phenomenally seem to me now, in which case there would indeed be trouble for the current version of representationalism. However, given that the memory image is representationally inaccurate, this assumption may reasonably be questioned. The representationalist who is an externalist of the nonteleological type distinguished earlier will certainly deny it; and no supporting argument is provided by Block. It seems to me that if anyone is begging the question here, it is Block himself.

Of course, the above response commits the representationalist to supposing that large changes in the phenomenal character of experiences can occur that are inaccessible from the first-person perspective, which may seem rather counterintuitive. But the relevant changes are ones that occur through time, not at a single time, and they only occur in switching cases. Arguably, the core intuition here is only that within a single context, a single external setting, no unnoticeable changes in phenomenal character can occur.[20]

The upshot, I suggest, is that Block has *not* shown that the representationalist cannot steer a safe course between the Scylla of Inverted Earth and the Charybdis of Swampman.

6.3   The Real Trouble with Biting the Bullet

All is not now plain sailing, alas. Unfortunately, an obstacle remains, not discussed by Block, that really does give the representationalist who adopts the strategy outlined in the last section an insurmountable problem.

The obstacle I have in mind concerns the transition from sensorily representing the clear sky as blue to sensorily representing it as yellow. In the case of the person who travels from Earth to Twin Earth, the content of his thoughts shifts *gradually*. Initially, he thinks that water is wet; after sufficient time on Twin Earth, he thinks that twater is wet. In the transition period, after some time on Twin Earth but before he becomes fully embedded in the new environment, he has thoughts whose contents neither determinately involve water alone nor determinately involve twater alone. Arguably, his thought is that either water or twater is wet. But the transition from thinking that water is wet to thinking that water or twater is wet is not itself a sharp one. And likewise, in the case of the transition from thinking that water or twater is wet to thinking that twater is wet.

According to the representationalist who accepts the present strategy, the clear sky on Inverted Earth initially looks blue to the traveler from Earth, but after sufficient time on Inverted Earth, the clear sky looks yellow to him. How does it look in between? What quality does the traveler then experience the clear sky as having? We can't say that during the transition period the sky looks blue *or* yellow. That seems unintelligible, given that blue and yellow are opposites on the hue circle.

It does not help us to say that the sky looks something *other than* blue or yellow in the transition period, since there seems no nonarbitrary way of specifying the relevant look. (It can hardly be the case that the sky looks first blue, then bluish-green, then green, then lime, then finally yellow. Why not say equally that it looks first blue, then purple, then red, then orange, and then finally yellow?) Moreover, the idea that the sky looks some *different* color than blue or yellow before full embedding in the new environment seems peculiar in the extreme anyway.

Note that the point just made about arbitrariness undermines the suggestion that the transition is extremely gradual, involving indistinguishable shifts in the apparent color of the sky. This would make the change in apparent color from blue to yellow unnoticeable to the traveler. But it leaves us with no way of saying which way around the hue circle the indistinguishable shifts are supposed to go.

The only alternative left seems to be to hold that the transition from looking blue to looking yellow is sudden and sharp so that the case isn't like the water/twater case at all. That seems quite counterintuitive, however, and cannot be reconciled with the account of sensory representation in terms of normal tracking. For there surely is no determinate time at which the traveler's sensory state goes from *normally* tracking blue to *normally* tracking yellow.

The conclusion I draw from these considerations is that there is *no* change in sensory representation with the move from Earth to Inverted Earth. What the representationalist requires, then, is an account of sensory representation that delivers this result not just for human beings but for swamp duplicates, too. That is the topic of the next section.

6.4   An Alternative Approach to Inverted Earth

In Tye (1995), I proposed a causal covariation account of the nonconceptual content of basic perceptual experiences. Such an account, I suggested, fitted well with the way in which these states are mechanically produced by our sensory systems in response to external stimuli. My claim was that for each sensory state, S, of a creature c, within the relevant set of alternative sensory states of c, we can define what S represents as follows:

S represents that P = df If optimal conditions were to obtain, S would be tokened in c if and only if P were the case; moreover, in these circumstances, S would be tokened in c because P is the case.[21]

I noted that optimal or normal conditions can vary, depending upon the kind of creature we are dealing with (whether the creature belongs to a species with an evolutionary history or a swamp duplicate). Now this account, however it is further elaborated, is essentially a counterfactual one. What matters is the tracking that *would* obtain under certain conditions, not the tracking that *actually* obtains.

The critical question, then, as far as determining the representational content of the traveler's experiences with the switch to Inverted Earth is whether, given the above proposal, the relevant counterfactuals travel with him. It seems to me plausible to suppose that they do. The Inverted Earth story essentially involves an artificial intervention in the operation of certain transducers. Inverting lenses are placed in the eyes of the traveler. These lenses reverse the way in which the light input is processed. Intuitively, the lenses *deceive* the traveler (in Block's original version of the story) so that when he first arrives, he has false beliefs on the basis of the phenomenal character of his visual experiences. He believes that the clear sky is blue, when really it is yellow. Of course, through time the traveler's beliefs adjust. But no matter how long he stays, it remains the case that the scientists from Inverted Earth have tampered with his visual transducers. Their operation is altered by the insertion of the lenses and, at no later time, is the system restored to its initial, natural state. The insertion of the lenses *interferes* with the operation of the sensory transducers. Accordingly, the transduction process is not in itself normal or optimal.

This is true not just for me, where the insertion of the lenses prevents my visual transducers from functioning as they were designed to do, but also for my swamp duplicate. In his case, there is still outside interference. Of course, Swamp Tye functions well after the interference in his new environment, but intuitively the lenses, considered in themselves, distort his color experiences. This distortion is masked by the color reversal on Inverted Earth, so that he cannot tell that he has been shifted to a very different environment, colorwise. But it is surely pretheoretically correct to say that his transducers have been interfered with.

Intuitively, then, it is true of the traveler's sensory state, as he looks at the clear sky on Inverted Earth (after however many years), that *had* there been no interference, that phenomenal state *would have been* causally correlated (in him) with blue things. Accordingly, by the causal covariation proposal, the traveler's sensory state continues to represent the clear sky as *blue*.

In effect, the present proposal is that the "optimal conditions" qualification in the above account of sensory representation is a *ceteris paribus* clause. It functions in much the same way as the implicit *ceteris paribus* clauses in such counterfactual-supporting generalizations as "Dropping stones causes them to fall to earth" and "Mixing an acid and a base produces a salt." These lawlike generalizations have exceptions when something interferes—for example, when the stones are attached to helium balloons or the beaker is dropped. But such exceptions do not falsify the generalizations. In these cases, *ceteris* is not *paribus*. Likewise, for the example of Inverted Earth.

It might now be suggested that the following objection arises: Suppose that Swamp Tye materializes on Earth with the inverting lenses as part of his visual apparatus.[22] Suppose further that Swamp Tye is immediately whisked off to Inverted Earth before he has a chance to experience any chromatic colors on Earth. (Imagine that he materializes at night and leaves for Inverted Earth before morning.) In this case, no outside interference with respect to his transducers occurs. Lenses aren't placed in Swamp Tye's eyes by the visiting scientists. They are there already. All the scientists do is to take Swamp Tye to their planet. In this case, one might urge, there is no reason to deny that *ceteris* is *paribus*. Thus, on the proposed account, Swamp Tye's experience, as he views the clear sky on Inverted Earth, represents yellow. That, however, seems counterintuitive; moreover, the suggestion that what it is like for Swamp Tye will vary, depending upon whether the lenses were in place from the start or inserted by others, seems absurd.

Let me begin my reply by making some further general remarks about the *ceteris paribus* clause, as I understand it. When *ceteris* is *paribus* for perceptual experiences, ideal perceptual conditions obtain. In the case of evolved creatures, it is natural to hold that such conditions for vision involve the various components of the visual system operating as they were designed to do in the sort of external environment in which they were designed to operate. Here, there is no interference—no genetic abnormalities to throw things off, no peculiarities in the outside setting. Everything is as it should be.

In the case of swamp duplicates, ideal perceptual conditions obtain again when there is no interference. But now design is irrelevant. In the case that the scientists insert inverting lenses, there is obviously interference. The processing that takes place afterward in the swamp creatures' visual systems interferes with the production of accurate color experiences. The same is true, I maintain, for swamp creatures that are duplicates of humans except for the additional inverting lenses, even if the lenses materialize with the creature. Here is why.

I argued at the end of the last section that there is simply no room for a plausible representational transition at the sensory level. This argument applies quite generally to humans and swamp creatures. At the nonconceptual sensory level, the quality the traveler first experiences on Inverted Earth, as he views the clear sky, is the same as the one he experiences after having been there for many years. In the case of human beings, this quality is blue. What about swamp duplicates? Consider Swamp Tye on Earth before the move to Inverted Earth, with the lenses in place. Granted, in the above case, he does not see any blue things in daylight. But if he had done so, how would they have looked to him? The answer clearly is that they would have looked yellow. For Swamp Tye would have called these things 'yellow' and he would have been puzzled by the apparent changes in the colors of things (given his phenomenal 'memories' of their colors). He would thus have experienced yellow where I (lacking lenses) experience blue.[23] Similarly, were Swamp Tye (with lenses) to have seen something yellow, he, unlike me, would have experienced blue. The quality Swamp Tye experiences, then, upon arrival on Inverted Earth as he sees yellow things (e.g., the clear sky) is blue.

So, given the lenses, whatever their origin, Swamp Tye's sensory system *mis*represents colors on Inverted Earth, just as it would have done on Earth had he stayed there. The processing that goes on in his visual system is not *optimal*. That processing *interferes* with the production of accurate color experiences. *Ceteris* is not *paribus* after all. Once again, there is no difficulty for the representationalist.

The remaining question for the representationalist who adopts this response to the Inverted Earth/Swampman problem concerns whether the causal covariation account of sensory representation presented above needs any further qualification. I am inclined to think that it does for the following reason. Suppose that sensory state S causally covaries with perceptible quality P under optimal conditions. Suppose, moreover, that P is nomically correlated with imperceptible quality Q. Then, according to the presented account, sensory state S represents not just P but also Q. However, if Q is imperceptible, it cannot contribute directly to the phenomenal look of a thing. And that spells trouble for the representationalist.

The problem is not restricted to the case of sensory representation. The hair shedding of cats (under normal conditions) is causally correlated with the lengthening of days; and lengthening days correlate (roughly) with increasing temperature. Thus, shedding in cats causally covaries with both day length and temperature. Even so, given what we know of the relevant biological mechanisms, it seems wrong to say that the shedding of hair represents temperature as well as (or instead of) day length.[24]

In the cat case, the causal covariation between the shedding of hair and increasing temperature arises because the hair shedding causally covaries with day length and day length covaries with temperature. Were the covariation link between temperature and day length broken (by, for example, keeping cats indoors at a constant temperature or moving them to higher altitudes at the same latitude), the hair shedding would continue to covary with day length (albeit artificial day length for the indoor case generated by varying the hours of artificial light), but not with temperature. For this reason, hair shedding is best taken to represent day length.

Intuitively, then, what is needed to supplement the basic causal covariation approach is a further asymmetric dependence condition. For state S to represent feature F not only must S causally covary with F under optimal conditions but it must also be the case that if there is some other feature G such that F covaries with G under optimal conditions then were F to fail to covary with G, the causal covariation link between S and F under optimal conditions would still hold but that between S and G would be broken.

This qualification handles the case of sensory state S covarying with both perceptible quality P and imperceptible quality Q. S can be held to represent P and not Q so long as it is held that were the covariation link between P and Q broken, S would continue to covary causally with P but not with Q.[25]

So far as I can see, then, the representationalist has an entirely satisfactory way of slipping between the horns of the Swampman/Inverted Earth dilemma. As long as an account of sensory representation of the sort sketched above is accepted, a safe path can be found. No unnecessarily large bullets need be swallowed. No strong intuitions need be ignored or rejected.

Notes

1. Again, of the externalist sort. Here, and subsequently, I leave out the qualifier for ease of exposition.

2. Your body pigments are also changed.

3. Block (1990) also describes a further Inverted Earth inversion. Suppose on Earth you have a molecule-by-molecule duplicate whom you leave behind when you depart for Inverted Earth. According to Block, after sufficient time has passed, your states will remain phenomenally identical to those your twin is undergoing on Earth, but they will be intentionally inverted.

4. I do not believe that this objection is absolutely decisive. Although Dretske nowhere takes his version of strong representationism to have the status of a necessary a posteriori truth, if it is true at all, he could do so. This would then allow him to argue that the discovery that he is a swamp creature would constitute an empirical refutation of strong representationalism.

5. Lycan (1996a, pp. 137–40) offers a reply to the Inverted Earth objection, which (by his own admission) assumes externalism for memory contents. (This reply is repeated in Lycan 1996b). No argument is offered; nor is any distinction drawn of the sort I discuss later between conceptual and phenomenal memory; and given the context in which Lycan's reply originally occurs (as a rejoinder to Block, myself, and several others), his discussion is, of necessity, rather brief—too brief, I suspect, to persuade those who are sympathetic to Block's objection. However, Lycan, in my view, is essentially correct in his response to Block, and there is, so far as I can tell, nothing in what I say to the various points that Block makes that is incompatible with his line. Where Lycan goes wrong, it seems to me, is in supposing not merely that he has answered Block but also that the line he takes is defensible *period*. That, in my view, is not the case (see section 6.3 in this chapter).

6. Lycan (*ibid*) calls the wide construal of memory content "standard" (1996a, p. 139) and "generally acknowledged" (1996b, p. 131); by a "wide construal," he means one in which present environment dictates content. This claim seems to me too strong. The most common view I have encountered is the one just described in which past environment is the decisive factor.

7. Suppose that instead of uttering the sentences mentioned earlier in the text, I am reading the sentences, "There is plenty of water around now. Water used to be in short supply, however. Unlike now, water in those days was a precious commodity." Suppose also that I am somewhat dubious about the veracity of their author, and I neither assent to nor dissent from what I am reading. The earlier points now go through for the case of thought rather than belief.

8. I concede that it would certainly be very counterintuitive, indeed obviously mistaken, for the externalist to claim that in the above example I remember that twater was not the only thing I used to drink before 5 PM, where the term 'remember' is being used as a success verb. But that, of course, is not the externalist's position.

9. For a more detailed discussion of objections and replies, see Tye (1998b).

10. The extension of Burge's Twin Earth case to memory is presented in Tye (1998b). For a discussion of phenomenal memory images, see pp. 129–33.

11. This example is also used in a discussion of privileged access in McLaughlin and Tye (1998).

12. See Reisberg (1987). Other pairs of faces Reisberg chose included Groucho Marx and Laurence Olivier, Humphrey Bogart and Burt Reynolds, Candice Bergen and Marilyn Monroe. Subjects were asked questions such as: Who has the longer face (relative to width)? Who has more closely set eyes? Who has a broader nose? Who has a more pointed chin? Who has a higher forehead? Who has bushier eyebrows?

13. However, there are important differences between memory images and pictures, even drawn ones. See discussion later in this chapter.

14. Many other experiments strongly suggest that visual images are not photographic but rather are constructed piecemeal with the aid of concept-driven processes; see Tye (1993) and Block (1983).

15. The example parallels that of Paul Boghossian (1994).

16. This is based on Block's assumption that visual experiences will switch their contents after a sufficiently long stay on Inverted Earth.

17. The symbolic view of phenomenal memory images does not entail that phenomenal memory is inherently conceptual. Not all symbols need be available for use in thought and belief. For a defense of the view that mental images generally have a partly matrix-like and partly symbolic structure—specifically, that they represent in the manner of symbol-filled arrays or matrices, see Tye (1991). For a related view, see Kosslyn (1980). The format of basic visual experiences is discussed in Tye (1995); see also Marr (1982).

18. Lycan (1996a) says the following about this passage: "The argument seems to be that the subject is justified in claiming introspective indistinguishability *across memories* (and hence indistinguishability obtains despite the representational shift)" (p. 139, my italics). This does not seem to me to be the argument at all. Insofar as introspective indistinguishability enters, it does so with respect to the subject's *present* visual experience of looking at the sky, and his memory of how the sky used to look.

19. It is worth stressing that if strong representationalism is true anywhere, then it should be true for phenomenal memory images because, trivially, such memory images are phenomenal states. They share phenomenal "feels" with perceptual experiences. If these "feels" of perceptual experiences are representational in nature, they must be representational whatever their bearers. So, any of a number of independent arguments for strong representationalism with respect to experience can be appealed to in support of the application of the view to the phenomenal character of phenomenal memory images.

20. For more on this issue, see Block 1998; also Tye 1998a.

21. Note the "if *and* only if" condition. Using a biconditional and not a single conditional is critical; the latter imposes much too weak a constraint.

22. Given the lenses, Swamp Tye isn't an exact duplicate of me. Minus the lenses, he is.

23. I assume here, of course, that my visual system is biologically normal so that things on Earth are typically as they visually appear to me (phenomenally).

24. I am indebted to Beth Preston here.

25. Jerry Fodor (1990) proposes an asymmetric nomic dependence account of representation. Fodor's concern, unlike mine, is with (simple) concepts. My proposal is importantly like Fodor's, however.

III

Color and Simple Minds

7

On Some Alleged Problems for Objectivism about Color

In their introduction to Simon Baron-Cohen's book *Mindblindness* (1995), two well-known cognitive scientists, Leda Cosmides and John Tooby, make the following remarks about color:

Just as common sense is the faculty that tells us that the world is flat, so too it tells us many other things that are equally unreliable. It tells us, for example, that color is out there in the world, an independent property of the objects we live among. But scientific investigations have led us, logical step by logical step, to escape our fantastically insistent, inelastic intuitions. As a result, we know now that color is not already out there, an inherent attribute of objects. We know this because we sometimes see physically identical objects or spectral arrays as having different colors—depending on background, circumstance, context—and we routinely see physically different spectral arrays as having the same color. The machinery that causes these experiences allows us to identify something as the same object across situations despite the different wavelength composites that it reflects from circumstance to circumstance. Far from being a physical property of objects, color is a mental property—a useful invention that specialized circuitry computes in our minds and then "projects onto" our percepts of physically colorless objects. This invention allows us to identify and interact with objects and the world far more richly than we otherwise could. That objects seem to be colored is an invention of natural selection, which built into some species, including our own, the specialized neural circuitry involved. (Cosmides and Tooby, 1995, p. xi)

The view that modern science leaves no place for colors in the objective world, notwithstanding the testimony of common sense to the contrary, is one with a long history.[1] Descartes and Galileo, for example, maintained that colors exist only in sensation, in the minds of perceivers, even though common sense holds otherwise. Science, they supposed, drives us to the conclusion that colors are really intrinsic properties of states of perceivers, properties that the ordinary person mistakenly conceptualizes as belonging to mind-independent things.

This view has exerted a powerful pull on twentieth-century philosophers, and it continues to do so today. Indeed, it was one consideration in the development of the infamous sense-datum theory. For if things in the real world lack color, but we experience things as colored, then the only way to *avoid* the conclusion that there is a deep and pervasive error in our color experience is to claim that the things we experience are not outside the mind at all (Russell 1912). Instead, they are mental objects or sense data. These are the real bearers of experienced color (Jackson 1977).

Projectivism of the sort recently espoused by Boghossian and Velleman (1989) is another descendant of the Descartes/Galileo view. Their position is that colors are really intrinsic properties of subjective sensory fields (akin to sense data) that perceivers mistakenly project upon things outside the mind. Thus, like Descartes and Galileo, they embrace the conclusion the classical sense-datum theorists repudiated—that "the best interpretation of color experience ends up convicting it of widespread and systematic error" (1989, p. 82).

A similar view is held by Larry Hardin (1988, 1997). What Hardin stresses as a particular difficulty for those who insist that common sense and science are not fundamentally at odds over color is the binary/unitary structure of the hues. Orange, for example, is a binary hue, namely, reddish-yellow, but red is unitary. Hardin comments:

. . . the unitary-binary structure of the colors as we experience them corresponds to no known physical structure lying outside nervous systems that is causally involved in the perception of color. This makes it very difficult to subscribe to a color realism that is supposed to be about red, yellow, green, blue, black, and white—that is, the colors with which we are perceptually acquainted. (1997, p. 300)

In this chapter, I want to examine the charge that there is no room in the objective world for color. In particular, I want to defend the view that colors are objective, physical properties against the criticisms brought by Cosmides, Tooby, and Hardin. I do not take this defense to secure color realism since other objections must also be faced. But I hope to show at least that the considerations adduced above should not persuade us to give up the position.

The chapter is divided into five sections. Section 7.1 summarizes the commonsense view of color. Section 7.2 considers three different positions on the nature of color, each of which is consistent with common sense, but only one of these survives close scrutiny. Section 7.3 offers a physicalist reply to the Cosmides and Tooby argument. Section 7.4 focuses on the division into unitary and binary hues. The final section, 7.5, presents some criticisms of alternative positions that repudiate the commonsense view.

7.1 The Commonsense View of Color

The obvious view of color, at least as far as common sense goes, is that the colors we see objects and surfaces to have are observer-independent properties of those objects and surfaces. We think of colors as inhering in surfaces, as, for example, in the case of the red that covers the outside of my car. We also think of colors as sometimes attaching to volumes, as in the case of the green that fills a piece of transparent green glass, or to thin films, as in the case of the blue of the sky. We take it for granted that objects typically retain their colors when they are not seen, thereby helping us to reidentify them.

Another important fact about color, which is manifest to us in our everyday life, is color constancy. Objects do not typically appear to change their colors during the day as the sunlight changes. Grass in the early morning looks to have the same color as it does at midday or late in the afternoon, even though the light is very different. Nor does it make much difference to the perceived colors of objects—plants, for example—when they are moved from outdoors to a setting of illumination by incandescent lamps. Moreover, wearing sunglasses has little effect on the colors objects appear to have (Hilbert 1987).

Constancy in apparent color, I might add, is sufficiently robust that two objects with different colors can continue to appear as they normally do even when they reflect light to the eye of the very same spectral composition. For example, a bluish object lit only by reddish light of the setting sun continues to look blue, and a reddish object illuminated by the bluish light of the sky continues to look red even though the light the objects reflect back to the eye is the same (Shepard 1997).

The fact that objects appear to retain the same color through a wide variety of changes in illumination conditions (though certainly not all) strongly suggests that colors are illumination-independent properties of those objects. The simplest, most straightforward explanation of color constancy is that the surfaces of colored objects have features that remain the same as the illumination conditions change—features that are represented in our color experiences and that are responsible for the sameness in their phenomenal character.

The intuitive conception of colors, then, is one of mind-independent, illumination-independent properties. These properties belong primarily to surfaces, but they also are possessed by volumes and films.

7.2   Three Theories of Color Consistent with Common Sense

Consistent with the conception just sketched are three possible positions concerning the nature of color: emergentism, brute nonreductive physicalism, and reductive physicalism. Emergentism is the view that colors are simple qualities, distinct from any of the qualities posited by scientific investigation of the world (Broad 1923). These qualities happen to emerge once certain scientific properties are instantiated in things. They are nomologically linked to the scientific properties, but the relevant laws are not metaphysically necessitated by the microphysical facts and laws. Thus, the emergentist concedes that there is a possible world just like the actual world microphysically but in which objects have different colors from those they actually possess or even no colors at all.

For the emergentist, there is no difficulty in reconciling modern science with commonsense about color. Color is not the sort of quality that science investigates. The various hues (or at least the unitary ones) are simple qualities whose natures are wholly given to us in sense experience. They are no more than they appear, and since they appear to be mind-independent qualities of things, that is what they are.

One obvious (and to my mind decisive) difficulty for emergentism is that it makes colors causally inefficacious. If colors might have been different or missing while the microphysical facts and laws remained the same, then which colors objects have or indeed whether they have any colors makes no difference to their physical interactions. But that intuitively is false. Painting the walls of a room yellow causes it to be brighter than it would be if the walls were painted brown. Staring at a bright red light and looking away causes a green afterimage. Moreover, if colors make no difference to how light is reflected from objects, to the subsequent changes at the retina, in the optic nerve, and so on, then it follows that we do not see colors![2] That seems absurd. Worse still, if we do not see colors, then, intuitively, we do not see things at all. Intuitively, we see the facing surfaces of things by seeing their colors.

Brute nonreductive physicalism differs from emergentism in one respect: it is now denied that there is a possible world just like our world microphysically but differing from it with respect to the distribution of colors.[3] For the brute nonreductive physicalist, there are synchronic bridge laws that link the microphysical realm with color, but these bridge laws are themselves metaphysically necessitated by the microphysical facts and laws. They obtain in all the possible worlds that are microphysical duplicates of our world.

This solves the problem of causal efficacy for colors. Unfortunately, it does so at the cost of creating another deep problem. The bridge laws are epistemically basic—there is no explanation as to how or why satisfaction of their antecedents brings about satisfaction of their consequents—and yet metaphysically derivative (determined as they are by the microphysical facts and laws). This seems very implausible. Everyone agrees that *some* laws are epistemically basic—in particular the fundamental microphysical laws—but to claim that there are laws that are epistemically basic *and* metaphysically derivative is to adopt a seemingly unstable position. If the laws are metaphysically derivative, then surely it *cannot* just be a brute fact that they obtain in the range of possible worlds that they do. Surely there must be some explanation.

The third position—reductive physicalism—is the view that colors are physical properties whose natures are discoverable by empirical investigation. This is not to say that colors have a microphysical nature. Rather, the claim is that they have a nature that is specifiable by some science. On this view, the synchronic bridge laws connecting the microphysical realm to color are both metaphysically derivative and epistemically nonbasic. They obtain in all possible worlds that duplicate our world microphysically and there is an explanation as to why this should be so—an explanation that allows us to understand how the microphysical facts necessitate the facts about color.

This view seems to me the only plausible view to take of color.[4] Unfortunately, according to Cosmides, Tooby, Hardin, and others, it cannot be reconciled with the commonsense conception of color. For their claim is that there are no physical properties with which colors, as ordinarily conceived, may be identified. In the next section I want to investigate this charge as it is developed by Cosmides and Tooby.

7.3 A Physicalist Reply to Cosmides and Tooby

Cosmides and Tooby adduce two considerations in defense of the view that colors are not mind-independent properties of external things. The first of these is that "we sometimes see physically identical objects or spectral arrays as having different colors" and the second is that "we routinely see physically different spectral arrays as having the same color" (1995, xi). I begin with the second.

In section 7.1, I noted that perceived or apparent color is invariant over a wide range of changes in illumination. In this context, I mentioned the case of the bluish object seen in the reddish light of the setting sun that continues to look blue, and the case of a plant that continues to look the same color even though it is moved from sunlight to indoor illumination by fluorescent lamps. These examples show that the spectral composition of the light reflected back to the eye at a given time does not determine experienced color at that time: items can reflect back different wavelengths of light at different times and yet appear to have the same color.

Cosmides and Tooby are correct to say that cases of this sort are routine. Clearly, however, it does not follow that colors are not mind-independent. What follows is simply that the color a surface has is not one and the same as the wavelength of the light it reflects under any particular illumination. That, it seems to me, is the true moral of color constancy.

What about the other consideration Cosmides and Tooby adduce—that physically identical things sometimes appear different colors, depending upon background conditions, and so forth? This merits careful examination.

Color constancy, as I have described it thus far, is illumination-invariant constancy. It is not what might be called "surround-invariant" constancy. Contrast effects for color are quite common and they have a significant influence on experienced color. In the cases of white, gray, black, and brown, these effects are very strong. For example, in figure 7.1, the annulus with the white column superimposed on top is the same shade of gray throughout, but it certainly does not appear that way, given the different backgrounds on the left and right sides of the column.

Even more strikingly, a uniform brown expanse such as is found in a bar of chocolate appears yellow when viewed through a narrow tube lined with black velvet! Here the very dark surrounding field supplied by the tube drastically changes the perceived color. The same phenomenon occurs when the chocolate is viewed through a pinhole in a black card.

Simultaneous contrast effects also occur for the hues red, yellow, green, and blue as well as their perceptual mixtures, although they are not so pronounced. For example, in one standard textbook demonstration of color constrast, a gray square on a red background appears greenish but the same square against a green background appears reddish. A yellow

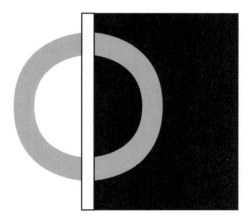

Figure 7.1
The apparent color of the annulus is different on the two sides of the superimposed white column.

stimulus placed in the center of a green background field appears somewhat more reddish than against a gray background. A blue stimulus centered on a red background appears more greenish.

There seem to me two possible ways to deal with these cases consistent with color realism of a commonsense sort. One is to agree with Cosmides and Tooby that in some cases physically identical objects do indeed have different colors. The color of an object is not (or at least is not always) just a function of its intrinsic properties. Given this view, where Cosmides and Tooby go wrong is in their subsequent reasoning. It just does not follow that external objects lack mind-independent colors.

To appreciate this point, consider the case of weight. How heavy something is depends upon its setting. Something very heavy on earth is light on the moon. The same obtains for motion. Something moving relative to my frame of reference is stationary relative to its own frame. Weight and motion are relational properties. Similarly, it may be suggested, in the case of color. The color a surface has is relative to a surround.[5] Thus, the fact that surroundings strongly influence color does *not* show that colors are really in the mind.

Perhaps it will be objected that it is part of commonsense thinking that colors are not relational. So, common sense and science remain in conflict. We may agree here that ordinary color concepts—the concepts we mobilize in our commonsense color thinking—are not relational concepts. In everyday life, when we think of something as brown, say, we do not typically think of it as bearing a relation to anything. But the fact that ordinary color concepts are not relational is perfectly compatible with supposing that their referents—the colors themselves—have relational natures.

Still, it may be insisted, the relational view of color (or at least some colors, e.g., the achromatic ones) surely goes against ordinary color *experience*. When, for example, a rubber ball looks blue to me, I experience blueness all over the facing surface of the ball. Each perceptible part of the ball looks blue to me. And none of these parts, in looking blue, look to me to have a relational property. On the contrary, it may be said, I experience blueness as intrinsic to the surface, just as I experience the shape of the surface as intrinsic to it. This simple fact is one that relational approaches to color cannot accommodate without supposing that a universal illusion is involved in normal experiences of color—that colors are really relational properties even though we experience them as nonrelational.

Is it obvious that we experience colors as nonrelational? It is certainly true that we do not experience colors *as* relational. Something, in looking blue to me, does not look to stand in some relation to something else. But it does not follow from this that something, in looking blue to me, looks to have a nonrelational property. Consider again the case of weight (first mentioned in chapter 5). The bar of gold feels very heavy as I lift it. In feeling heavy, it does not feel to have a relational property. Does it feel *not* to have a relational property? If so, there is a grand illusion in our experiences of weight. Better to say surely that the bar does not feel not to have a relational property—that our experience leaves open the nature of the property involved.

There are other plausible examples. Intuitively, something experienced as moving is not experienced as moving relative to the perceiver's frame of reference. The latter is not part of the phenomenology of something's appearing to move. Intuitively, something that is experienced as large—something that looks large—does not look phenomenologically to involve a certain reference class. Arguably, then, colors can be relational even though their relational character is not revealed in color experience.

Still, I must confess that I am not satisfied by this response. Intuitively, it seems to me, our ordinary experiences of color place (many[6]) object colors on the surfaces of objects independently of what is going on elsewhere in the surroundings. In this respect, color seems to me like shape. We experience the redness of a ripe tomato as not involving anything *away* from the facing surface of the tomato as being a *local* feature of that surface, just as we do its shape. To take a relational view of color is to repudiate this commonsense fact.[7]

A second reply to Cosmides and Tooby is to note that background effects are not uncommon for shape. Consider, for example, the following cases: In figure 7.2, the vertical rectangle appears to have slightly bowed sides; in figure 7.3 the circle and the square appear distorted. We don't conclude from these cases that shape is not an intrinsic physical

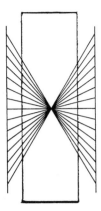

Figure 7.2
A variation on the Hering figure.

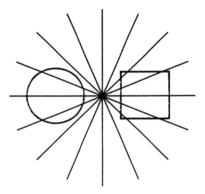

Figure 7.3
Orbison figure (two combined).

property of external things. Rather, we say that the cases are illusions or normal misperceptions induced by the background setting. Why, then, should we not say the same sort of thing with respect to color? On this view, the fact that no single intrinsic physical property is common to all objects that are experienced as having the same color by normal perceivers in standard conditions of illumination is not in the least threatening to color realism.

Admittedly, simultaneous contrast effects are more common for color than for shape. But our ordinary description of these cases usually involves an appearance/reality distinction just as it does for the counterpart cases involving shape. We say that the blue swatch of cloth *appears* greenish against the red background, that the yellow patch of paint *appears* reddish against a green background, and so on. We don't normally say that the swatch *is* greenish in the former context or that the paint *is* reddish in the latter. Neither the swatch of cloth nor the patch of paint changes its color or acquires a new color as the background changes. The swatch is still blue, the paint still yellow.

Likewise, if I have a gray jacket and I cut out a small piece that subsequently looks white to me as I hold it against a black sheet of paper, I don't infer that it *is* now white. After all, if later I reattach the material to the original jacket, I don't think of it as having changed its color twice in the interim—from gray to white and then back to gray again! That simply isn't how we ordinarily individuate real color changes.

Here is another example of simultaneous color contrast (Hurvich 1981). The French chemist, Chevreul, was the director of dyes at a tapestry works from 1824 to 1883. He wrote of the problems he had in convincing buyers of calicos with red and black patterns that the black dye used was really pure. The buyers often complained that the dye in the cloth was of inferior quality and tinged with green instead of being black as ordered. The only way Chevreul found to persuade the buyers that they were not being cheated was to place specially designed paper cutouts of uniform reflectance over the calicos so that the red parts could no longer be seen, thereby revealing the black parts without any greenish cast. As the buyers came to realize, a subtle illusion was at work: the green tint was merely apparent, the result of a contrast effect.

That simultaneous contrast effects involve illusions is a point that color irrealists themselves admit. For example, Hardin (1997) makes the following remark:

The colors experienced in after-images, colored shadows, and simultaneous contrast, are explicable in terms of the operation of nervous systems and cannot plausibly be supposed to exist apart from them. (p. 289)

It seems to me that Hardin is right to the following extent: the colors things are *experienced* as having as a result of the contrast between the real color of the stimulus and the real color of the background are merely apparent. They do not really exist. Our experiences represent them as being instantiated when in reality they are not. Such colors *on such occasions* are mere intentional inexistents. That simultaneous color contrast, understood in this way, is produced by, and explicable in terms of, the workings of the visual system (e.g., by opponent processing[8]) is something no color realist need deny.

A further point is worth making here about simultaneous color contrast. It is very natural to see cases of such contrast as being importantly like cases of successive color contrast.[9] The latter occur in afterimaging and involve opponency through time as opposed to space.[10] For example, if you stare at a red light and look at a white sheet of paper afterward, you will experience a green afterimage. Similarly, if you attend for a minute or so to a white dot placed in the center of a picture of the American flag with its colors inverted, and then focus your eyes on a white sheet of paper, you will experience the flag again, this time in its normal colors.

In these cases, it seems clear that an illusion is present. The experienced shape does not really exist. When one sees an afterimage, there is nothing that one sees. The term 'see' here has a phenomenal sense that lacks existential import. It is the sense that is in play when we say that the man suffering from delirium tremens sees pink rats. Seeing a green, round afterimage consists of having a certain kind of visual experience. The experience isn't green or round. Rather, it is an illusory experience as of something green and round (from here), something filmy and hovering in space. In the flag example, nothing really has the colors, red, white, and blue; it simply appears to one that these colors are present. Analogously, in the case of simultaneous color contrast. Nothing really is green when the blue stimulus is experienced against the red background. It just appears that way.

Perhaps it will be objected that the account just offered of simultaneous color contrast threatens to generate a selective irrealism about colors. For white, gray, black, and brown, it is often said, are pure contrast colors. If contrast effects involve color illusions, then nothing in the external environment has any of these colors.

To evaluate this objection, we need to understand what it is for something to be a pure contrast color. According to Irving Rock (1983, p. 503), a pure contrast color is one that can only be seen if "certain specific conditions of contrasting luminances . . . obtain." Rock claims that if one is presented with a situation in which there is completely uniform stimulation throughout the whole field of view, the field does not look white or gray or black or brown. Rather, "one has the impression of looking into a diffuse, three-dimensional fog" (Rock, p. 503). This field (called a "Ganzfield") is one in which no contours whatsoever are visible. The field may appear dim or bright but, in Rock's view, it does not look to have a definite color at all.

Prima facie, this is a puzzling position. Consider the case in which one is in a totally dark room. As Rock notes, this "can be considered to be a special case of a Ganzfield." However, he insists, "a dark room looks dark, not black" (p. 503).

This view seems to me stipulative. After all, in ordinary life, we certainly say things like "It's pitch black in here" with respect to totally dark rooms, presumably because that is the way such rooms look to us. Let us, then, distinguish between black and BLACK. In the dark room, one experiences black but not BLACK.[11] Something is BLACK, let us say, just in case it is black and it is darker than its surroundings. BLACK, thus, is a pure contrast color, but black is not. Even so, irrealism about BLACK does not follow. For something can look BLACK in a given setting and genuinely be BLACK (so long as it is black and darker than its surroundings). Of course, the onus is still upon us to say in what black consists. But of that, more shortly.

On this proposal, BLACK is a compound, partly relational property. One sees the BLACKNESS of an object indirectly by seeing its blackness and seeing its relative darkness with respect to its surroundings. But black is not relational, or at least no compelling reason has yet been given for supposing that it is. Similarly, WHITE and GRAY are compound, partly relational properties, but white and gray are not.[12] One experiences whiteness without also experiencing WHITENESS in the case that one places half a white ping-pong ball over each eye and illuminates the two halves from outside by a white light. Grayness is experienced without GRAYNESS in the case that one stares into an enveloping gray mist (and perhaps also when one views a detuned televison screen that fills one's visual field).

What about the case of brown? Brown normally is experienced where there is contrast (Gregory 1977), but it seems to me false to assert unequivocally that one cannot experience brown without an appropriate contrast.[13] Consider, for example, the case in which one is surrounded by a light brown fog. Of course, in such a Ganzfield, the brown will "wash out" of one's phenomenal field very quickly. But then the same is true for colors such as red and blue.[14] So, while much is puzzling about the nature of the color brown, nothing in the objection we are considering should lead us to deny that soil and shoes, for example, are ever really brown.[15]

So far I have concentrated upon background effects. What about cases in which there is a change in apparent color in virtue of a change in the viewing distance or the viewing apparatus? Blood, for example, looks red to the naked eye, but yellow under a microscope. Mountains do not look the same color when viewed close up as they do from several miles away (Jackson and Pargetter 1997). An expanse of color in a cartoon strip may look orange from a distance but red and yellow at close proximity (Block 1990).

The obvious reply is that changing the viewing apparatus or viewing distance changes the size of the minimum visible area. Parts of the object not visible from afar or without the viewing apparatus become visible close up or under a microscope. A drop of blood is red to the naked eye, as are all those parts of the drop that one can discern with the eye alone. What is yellowish is a smaller part, namely that part seen under the microscope. Likewise, as one walks toward a mountain, the greens and browns one comes to see are features of parts of the mountain one could not see before—for example, the wooded region on one of the lower slopes. Since one is seeing a part or parts not previously visible in the two cases, the fact that the color changes is no threat to the objectivity of color.

The same is true in the case of the expanse of color in the comic strip. Part of the expanse is red and part is yellow. Those parts are not visible at a distance. When they become visible, the former part looks red and the latter looks yellow. Neither part ever looks orange. The expanse *as a whole* is orange and it looks that way. The expanse as a whole does not look red and neither does it look yellow. If someone remarks that the expanse looks (or is) red and yellow close up, all that is meant surely is that *part* of the expanse looks (is) red and *part* looks (is) yellow.

This is not to deny that in some cases, the color a thing looks to have is different from the color it really has even if the lighting conditions are normal. From a great distance, mountains often appear purplish. This seems best treated as a color illusion, on a par with a chiliagon's looking round when viewed from a considerable distance.

The question remains: with which external physical properties are colors to be identified, given the second response to Cosmides and Tooby? The obvious objectivist proposal here for surface color appeals to surface reflectance, independent of background. In the case of white, for example, what matters is not the total quantity of light reflected but the percentage. Although a sheet of white paper in the shade reflects much less light than a black object in sunlight, the white object reflects a much, much higher proportion of the incident light. What prototypical white surfaces have in common is a very high, constant, diffuse reflectance percent.[16] They reflect back in a diffuse manner roughly 80 percent or more of the incident light, whatever its wavelength. White objects that are whiter than other white objects have a higher uniform reflectance. An ideal white object diffusely reflects 100 percent of the light that strikes it.

Black objects, by contrast, reflect an extremely low, constant percentage of the illuminant for all wavelengths (below roughly 10 percent).[17] An ideal black object absorbs all the incident light: none is reflected. Gray objects have intermediate reflectances. Moreover, like white and black objects, they reflect (roughly) the *same* percentage of incident light, whatever the wavelength. Some grays, of course, are darker or whiter than others, depending upon how close they are to the reflectance range for white things. A perfectly gray card that reflects roughly 20 percent of any illuminating light (Westphal 1987) has a dull color.[18]

In the case of the hues red, yellow, green, and blue, the phenomenon of metamerism makes things more complicated. Evidently, restrictions need to be placed on the type of reflectance that is relevant. One way to try to impose the restrictions for the hues is via conditions that incorporate some of the insights of the opponent process theory without thereby adopting a subjectivist view of color. Consider, for example, the simplified quantitative model of opponent processing presented by Hardin (1988). According to Hardin, chromatic color experience is generated by neuronal activity in two channels, one for red-green color experience and the other for yellow-blue. Where '0' represents the base level of neural activity—that is, the level corresponding to no visual response—and 'L', 'M', and 'S' represent the neural activity in the relevant neurons connecting to the long, medium, and short wavelength cones in the eye, the difference in L and M activity yields the red-green channel while the sum of L and M activity minus the S activity gives the yellow-blue channel. Specifically, where (L-M) is the red-green signal,

$(L - M) > 0$ yields the experience of (pure) red

and

$(L - M) < 0$ yields the experience of (pure) green,

assuming the yellow-blue channel is in balance. Similarly, where $(L + M)$ − S is the yellow-blue signal,

$(L + M) - S > 0$ yields the experience of (pure) yellow

and

$(L + M) - S < 0$ yields the experience of (pure) blue,

assuming the red-green channel is in balance.

This model is oversimplified, as Hardin notes, since the above formulae should be assigned coefficients that correspond to appropriate weightings for the three cone types (corresponding to the proportions of each cone type in a given retinal region, the relative efficiency of each cone type in generating an output from the radiant energy, and so on). However, it suffices for present purposes.

On the reasonable assumption that, *ceteris paribus*, our color experiences under normal viewing conditions are veridical, we may now propose that a surface is (pure) red, for example, so long as it has a reflectance that, *ceteris paribus*, under normal viewing conditions, enables it to reflect light that produces opponent processing distinctive of the experience of (pure) red.[19] More directly, where L^* is the amount of long wavelength light, M^* is the amount of middle wavelength light, and S^* is the amount of low wavelength light (corresponding to the neural activity, L, M, and S respectively), we may conjecture that a surface is (pure) red iff it has a reflectance that allows it *ceteris paribus*, under normal viewing conditions, to reflect light such that, for the reflected light, $M^* <_s L^*$ and $S^* =_a (M^* + L^*)$.[20] Parallel proposals can be constructed for the other hues.[21]

An additional point is important: any actual counterexample to this proposal will also be a counterexample to the opponent-processing model sketched above. Qualify the latter appropriately to handle the counterexample—it is, after all, by admission, oversimplified in certain respects—and the correspondingly qualified version of the former will handle the counterexample too. It is also worth noting that no claim is being made that there is, in nature apart from us, anything special about the relevant reflectances.[22] We find them special because of how our visual systems are constructed (Gibbard 1996). In this sense, colors are indeed anthropocentric, but their being so does not make them subjective. They are, I claim, real, objective properties, even if they are of no particular interest to creatures lacking our visual apparatus. The colors we see are tailored to the color detection system evolution has given us. The two fit one another like hand and glove.

Obviously questions remain here about how to spell out the proposal just outlined (and likewise for the relational account)—questions that go beyond the scope of this discussion.[23] However the story is developed, it may be insisted that a general conceptual difficulty attaches to *any* view that identifies colors with dispositions—even local, nonrelational dispositions to reflect light—namely that dispositions, unlike colors, are not properties of a sort that can be (directly) seen or otherwise experienced.

Consider, for example, the brittleness of a sheet of glass. Intuitively, that disposition is not (directly) experienced. It is inferred from how the glass looks and one's general knowledge. The same holds for, the elasticity of a rubber band. According to some philosophers (e.g., McGinn 1996), we (directly) experience only the manifestations of dispositions—the glass shattering, the rubber band stretching. We do not see the dispositions themselves.

It is certainly true that in some cases we do not experience dispositions. But is this really true in all cases? Consider the feeling of hardness as one grasps a lump of granite in one's hand. Hardness is a disposi-tion—the disposition to retain shape, to resist deformation against applied pressure. It seems to me not at all obvious that one does not directly experience the hardness of the granite. Of course, when one feels the hardness of something, the dispositional property is thereby mani-fested or exercised. But equally, when one sees the color of a surface, the relevant reflectance is manifested or exercised too, because a certain percentage of the incident light is reflected from the seen object to the eye.

The upshot, I suggest, is that there is no obvious pressing conflict between modern science and color. As yet, no compelling reason has been given for taking the view that the ordinary person is making a drastic mistake in thinking of colors as mind-independent properties of exter-nal objects and surfaces. Let us now consider whether the distinction between unitary and binary hues is more problematic for the color objectivist.

7.4   The Unitary/Binary Structure of the Hues

Some colors are unitary, in particular, red, yellow, green, blue, black, and white. Others are binary, for example, orange, pink, purple, and lime. Binary colors are always mixes of other colors. Orange is a reddish yellow, lime is a yellowish-green, purple a bluish red. Unitary colors have shades that are not mixes of other colors. Red, for example, has a shade that is not a combination of any other hues. This is unique red.

Hardin (1997) claims that the unitary/binary distinction creates deep trouble for any version of physicalism that identifies colors with exter-nal, physical properties. In his view, nothing about surface reflectances or any other physical structures outside the head that are involved in the production of color experiences can account for the division of colors into binary and unitary hues.

Before we can evaluate this objection to physicalism, we need to under-stand what is meant by saying that binary colors are mixes whereas unitary colors are not. Hardin clarifies this claim as follows:

Each of the Hering primaries is *unitary*, that is, contains no perceptible trace of any of the others, and this feature distinguishes them from the rest of the colors, such as . . . the oranges, which are *binary*, that is, perceptual mixtures of the elementary colors. . . . To say that orange is a *perceptual* mixture of red and yellow is not to refer to the way that orange pigment or lights are physically generated. This point is important, so let's consider it in more detail.

Suppose we project onto a screen two overlapping beams of light, one red, one green. The region of overlap will look yellow. Now let one of the beams be red, the other yellow. The region of overlap will look orange. In both instances, we have physically combined lights to produce a mixed color. The difference is that whereas the orange spot *looks* like a mixture of red and yellow, the yellow spot does not *look* like a mixture of red and green. . . .

Orange is, then, a perceptual mixture of red and yellow. (1997, p. 291)

Suppose we grant all these claims. What follows for physicalism? The answer, I suggest, is "Nothing troublesome whatsoever." Moreover, nothing troublesome follows for physicalism, even if we reject Hardin's perceptual account of the way in which orange is binary and we maintain instead that orange is a literal, nonperceptual mixture of red and yellow. This needs a little explanation.

Consider first Hardin's assumption that the commonsense view that orange is reddish-yellow is really a claim to the effect that orange looks like a mixture of red and yellow. Intuitively, that just does not seem right. The commonsense claim is that orange *is* reddish-yellow. Orange things *are* a bit reddish and they *are* also a bit yellowish—or so we pretheoretically believe. Hardin takes the line that this is clearly incompatible with physicalism (per the quotation on p. 146 above). But he is mistaken.

Let us assume again that the oversimplified opponent-processing model (Hardin 1988) is correct. Then the experience of red (not pure red) occurs iff $L - M > 0$, and the experience of yellow (not pure yellow) occurs iff $(L + M) - S > 0$. Now, let us agree with Hardin that, necessarily, when something looks orange, it looks red to a degree and it also looks yellow to a degree. Indeed, let us accept that looking orange is one and the same as looking reddish and also looking yellowish. To simplify the discussion that follows, let us further suppose that looking reddish is just looking red without looking pure red and likewise for the case of looking yellowish. Hardin's model now predicts that the experience of orange occurs iff $L - M > 0$ and $(L + M) - S > 0$.

My corresponding objectivist claim about surface orange is as follows: a surface is orange iff it has a reflectance that allows it, *ceteris paribus*, under normal viewing conditions, to reflect light such that, for the reflected light, $L^* >_s M^*$ and $(L^* + M^*) >_s S^*$. Since, on the proposed account, a surface is reddish (i.e., red but not pure red, as we are assuming) iff it has a reflectance . . . such that, for the reflected light, $L^* >_s M^*$, and a surface is yellowish iff it has a reflectance . . . such that, for the reflected light, $(L^* + M^*) >_s S^*$, orange is, quite literally, a mixture of reddishness and yellowishness. The first reflectance is constituted by the last two.

Note that this line of response does not commit the physicalist to holding that (pure) red is purply-orange. Looking purple is looking reddish and looking bluish. According to the model, the experience of blue (but not pure blue) occurs iff $(L + M) < S$. So, the experience of purple occurs iff $L > M$ and $(L + M) < S$. Accordingly, a surface is purple iff it has a reflectance that allows it, *ceteris paribus*, under normal viewing conditions, to reflect light such that $L^* >_s M^*$ and $(L^* + M^*) <_s S^*$. Evidently then (pure) red is not a literal mixture of purple and orange. Indeed, no color is. For no reflectance is such that it allows a surface to reflect light that satisfies incompatible conditions. (Pure) red, according to the proposed account, is not a literal mixture of any other colors at all.

This is my preferred response to the binary/unitary objection to physicalist realism about colors. But it should also be pointed out that there is no difficulty for the physicalist even if we understand the binary/unitary distinction in the way Hardin suggests. According to Hardin, orange is reddish-yellow in that necessarily something, in looking orange, looks reddish and looks yellowish. By contrast, yellow is not reddish-green, since it is not necessary that when something looks yellow, it looks red to any degree or green to any degree. For unique yellow, when something looks *that* shade, it does not look red or green to any degree. Looking yellow is not the same as looking red to some degree and looking green to some degree.[24]

Orange, then, is a perceptual mix of red and yellow but yellow is not a perceptual mix of red and green. But this the commonsense physicalist with respect to color can happily accept. For facts about perceptual mixture are best taken as facts about how colors are represented in color experience. In experientially representing something as orange, we represent it as being red to a degree and also as being yellow to a degree. However, there is a shade of yellow such that, in experientially representing something as having that shade (unique yellow), we do not represent it as being red to a degree and being green to a degree. Nor do we represent it as being orange to a degree and lime to a degree. Thus, the determinables, red and yellow, enter into the content of the experience of something's looking orange, whatever the shade of orange. But in the case of yellow, there is a shade such that the only determinable that enters into the content of something's looking that shade of yellow is yellow. This tells us that there is an important difference in how we represent orange and yellow in our color experiences, a difference that is naturally explicable in terms of opponent processing. But it presents no threat to the view that the colors orange and yellow are objective, physical properties of the same general type.[25]

Admittedly, on the assumption that our color experiences are generally veridical, the reply just offered entails that orange things *are* red to a degree and also yellow to a degree. That, however, is unproblematic for the reasons given earlier, if colors are reflectances of the sort I have sketched. Therefore, nothing in the binary/unitary distinction should lead us to give up the commonsense view of color.

7.5   Criticisms of Theories at Odds with Common Sense

I hope that I have succeeded in showing that it is not as easy to make the case that a deep tension exists between modern science and commonsense about color as is often supposed. Those who take the opposing view not only adopt a position that is very hard to believe but also encounter extremely serious difficulties of their own. The problems faced by the classical sense-datum theory are so familiar that I shall not repeat them again here. Instead, let me focus upon some objections to projectivism.

Projectivism, upon reflection, seems incomprehensible. The qualities we experience in seeing the colors of surfaces are experienced as qualities of those surfaces. They are qualities that we can only conceive of as qualities of spatially extended surfaces (or volumes or films). The suggestion made by Cosmides and Tooby (1995) as well as by Hardin (1988) that those qualities really belong to sensations or experiences seems unintelligible. Certainly, *I* can attach no sense to the claim that the redness I experience as covering the surface of a ripe tomato is really a property of my experience. As Shoemaker has noted (1994), one might as well say that properties like being even or being prime, properties of numbers, are really properties of material objects. The latter claims are category mistakes. So, too, it seems, is the former. Nor does it help to say, following Boghossian and Velleman (1989), that the qualities we experience in seeing colors are really qualities of subjective visual fields (or portions thereof). That, too, seems no easier to grasp; and with its reification of sensory fields, it faces the very same objections as the classical sense-datum theory.

An alternative possible projectivist view is one that denies that the qualities we experience in seeing colors are instantiated in anything at all.[26] They are neither qualities of external things nor are they qualities of inner experiences. We mistakenly project these qualities onto external things, but they are qualities without *any* real bearers. This view seems to me a *little* more appealing than the first version of projectivism. But it still seems deeply puzzling, even leaving to one side its counterintuitiveness. Since color qualities (or at least unitary color qualities) are now simple qualities that exist only in the intentional contents of experiences, there seems to be no satisfactory way of explaining *how* our experiences represent *those* qualities as instantiated. Indeed, we seem to have no grasp upon what it would take for such qualities *to be* instantiated, if they are never instantiated in actual fact. If, for example, nothing really is red, then what would it take for something to have redness? What conditions would a physical surface (or volume or film) have to meet to be red? I can see no satisfactory nonarbitrary answer to this question. So, it appears the conclusion to which this form of projectivism is driven is that redness *could* not be instantiated in a physical surface (or volume or film). Unfortunately, our concept of red, as noted above, is the concept of a quality of a spatially extended surface (or volume or film). Conceptually, we have no difficulty in grasping how redness could be instantiated. So, again projectivism seems incoherent.

It appears, then, that no one has yet succeeded in articulating a satisfactory alternative to the view that modern science and commonsense are compatible with respect to color. Unless further compelling objections are forthcoming, the best available hypothesis is that color is an objective, physical property of external things.[27]

Notes

1. A predecessor of this view is found in the writings of Democritus, according to whom the world is made up of colorless collections of atoms in the void.

2. I assume here that seeing X demands a causal connection with X.

3. John Campbell (1997) holds this view although he denies that it is a version of physicalism. (He calls his position the "Simple View."). The disagreement here is merely over how to use the term 'physicalism'. Since it is accepted that the microphysical facts determine all the facts about color, it seems to me best to classify the position as a physicalist one.

4. Two variants of this view are: rigid, reductive physicalism and nonrigid, reductive physicalism. On the latter position (defended by Jackson and Pargetter, 1997), color terms are nonrigid designators for physical properties. These terms pick out different physical properties in different possible worlds. They also sometimes refer to different physical properties within the same possible world. What the referents of the same color term in different possible worlds (or in different settings within a world) have in common is that they all are disposed to look the same way to normal perceivers in standard conditions. Accordingly, on this version of physicalism, it is a nonreductive, necessary truth that things that are red are disposed to look a certain way to normal perceivers in standard conditions.

The alternative, rigid version of physicalism holds that color terms are rigid designators for physical properties. Among its defenders are Armstrong (1997), Byrne and Hilbert (1997), and Smart (1997); see also Gibbard (1996), Tye (1995) Grandy (1989), Hilbert (1987), and Kripke (1972).

In the discussion that follows, my interest is in defending the second rigid version of physicalism against the objections of Cosmides, Tooby, and Hardin. For ease of exposition, I ignore the nonrigid view. For some objections directed against the thesis that colors are secondary qualities but also apply to the nonrigid version of physicalism, see the first, third, and fourth difficulties raised in note 27 below.

5. This suggestion was made to me in conversation by Fred Dretske.

6. More on this qualification later; see pp. 157–8.

7. Intuitions on this issue seem to differ. Those objectivists who disagree with me on this and who hold that colors are relative to surrounding settings (or at least some colors, e.g., the achromatic ones) must face the question of which

physical properties they are. The obvious place to look as far as surface colors go is in the ratio of reflectances that surfaces bear to their backgrounds (where the reflectance of a surface is given by its disposition to reflect a certain percentage of the incident light at each wavelength) or in the difference between such reflectances.

8. For an account of the opponent processing theory, see Hurvich (1981); also Hardin (1988).

9. I do not mean to deny that there are any significant differences between the two.

10. Note that Hardin mentions simultaneous color contrast cases in the same breath as the case of afterimaging in the quoted passage.

11. Does one see blackness in the totally dark room? In the phenomenological sense of the term 'see', the answer is "Yes" because one experiences blackness just as one does with respect to a part of one's visual field that is black in normal lighting conditions. One does not see blackness or anything black, in any sense of 'see' that requires light transmission. Arguably, 'see', in its usual success sense, has no such requirement. See Tye (1982).

12. Something is WHITE iff it is white and lighter than its surroundings. Something is GRAY iff it is gray and neither in very light or very dark surroundings.

13. Gregory makes no such strong claim himself.

14. For example, if the Ping-Pong ball halves I referred to earlier are illuminated by a red light, one initially has an experience of red, but in a very short time one sees no hue.

15. Brown, in my view, is a darkened yellow. This is not to say simply that it is a dark yellow (i.e., dark for a yellow). Dim yellows are dark but they are not brown. Browns are yellows of very low luminance—significantly lower than that of any items we would classify in everyday life as dark yellow in color.

16. Mirrors are not white since they do not have a very high *diffuse* reflectance percent. They reflect back a very high percentage of the incident light but, given their flatness, they have no tendency to spread out the reflected light in varying directions.

17. A totally dark room is *not* black, on this account. The remark, "It's pitch black in here," taken literally, is false. Nothing in the room really is pitch black. One who makes this remark is subject to an illusion.

18. Note that I am giving a (rough) account of white, black, and gray (not WHITE, BLACK, and GRAY).

19. The *ceteris paribus* qualification is included here because of contrast effects. These experiential effects interfere with or mask the real color.

20. Here '<ₐ' abbreviates "significantly less than' and '=ₐ' abbreviates "approximately the same as." I am influenced in making this proposal by a remark (left undeveloped into a general view) in Byrne and Hilbert (1997).

21. Proposals of this general sort are also to be found in Hilbert (1987), Grandy (1989), Tye (1995), and Gibbard (1996).

22. There is no difficulty for the reflectance account in allowing color to vary with viewing apparatus or viewing distance. As Hilbert (1987, pp. 122–25) notes, the reflectance of a surface, X, of uniform color can differ from the reflectances of some spatial parts of X, namely, those that are sufficiently small that they are not visible under normal viewing conditions for X.

23. One important issue concerns how to elucidate the notion of normal viewing conditions. It is sometimes suggested that the existence of individual color differences creates a real problem here. I am unconvinced. Think of the color visual system as a gauge of color. Given slight differences in how the color gauge is calibrated in different individuals, slightly different color perceptions result. Compare this with the measurement of length by various rulers, some more fine grained in their scales than others. Different rulers yield slightly different assessments of length but none need be *in*accurate. Each specifies length correctly, given its inherent limitations. Even so, some are *more* accurate or *more* sensitive than others, under conditions of normal use. See also chapter 4, case 7.

24. Again in the range greater than 0 and less than 1.

25. This reply is similar to one made by Byrne and Hilbert (1997), but it is not the same. They say:

Now any object that is visually represented as orange is also represented as having precisely two of these superdeterminables, reddishness and yellowishness (in fact, we may identify orange with *reddishness & yellowishness*). And any object that is visually represented as yellow is either represented as having greenishness and yellowishness, reddishness and yellowishness, or, in the case of unique yellow, only yellowishness. Thus, there is a shade of yellow such that any object represented as having that shade is represented as having just one superdeterminable, and no such shade of orange. This is our analysis of BINARY (the claim that yellow is unique and orange is binary). (1997, pp. 280–281).

This seems to me not quite right, even if we accept (as I do not) a perceptual 'looks' analysis of BINARY. Yellowishness is being yellow to a degree (less than 1 and greater than 0) or being borderline yellow. For if yellowishness is taken to be a broader quality (i.e., being yellow to a degree greater than 0), then orange cannot plausibly be identified with reddishness and yellowishness. However, things that are visually represented as unique yellow—as having that particular shade of yellow—are not represented as yellowish. On the contrary, they are represented as being fully yellow or pure yellow (yellow to degree 1). So, there is no superdeterminable that enters into the content of visual experiences as of unique yellow. It follows that the Byrne/Hilbert analysis of the claim that yellow is unitary fails.

26. A position of this sort seems to be held by John Mackie (1976).

27. It might be suggested that one alternative way of reconciling common sense and modern science on color is to adopt the view that colors are secondary

qualities, that is, dispositions to cause the appropriate experiences in normal perceivers in standard conditions. One objection to this view is that it seems viciously circular: the appropriate experience for the color F is surely the experience as of F. A second worry is that the view does not really comport with common sense, since it is part of common sense that colors are mind-independent properties like shape (see p. 147). A third difficulty is that there are imaginary counterexamples such as Kripke's killer-yellow (which is possessed by objects that kill anyone who looks at them). Fourthly, the view seems at odds with the actual facts. Cases of simultaneous color contrast occur to normal perceivers in standard conditions, and, as I argued earlier, the best interpretation of these cases takes them to involve illusions. The blue stimulus against the red background is not really greenish. It merely looks greenish to normal perceivers in standard conditions of illumination. These cases can be handled by introducing a *ceteris paribus* clause into the dispositionalist analysis, as can counterexamples of the killer-yellow sort (see Johnston, 1992). But there remains a further objection. Color irrealism is surely a conceptual possibility. It is surely conceptually possible that, for example, in actual fact nothing really is red even though, *ceteris paribus*, normal perceivers in daylight are subject to the experience of red. One might deny that this case is conceptually possible on the grounds that it is a conceptual truth that if red things do not look red to normal perceivers in daylight, then *ceteris* is not *paribus*. But what would justify the claim that this is indeed a *conceptual* truth? It seems to me that one would have to take "*ceteris paribus*" in the present context to mean something like: assuming things have the colors they appear to have. And that would make the dispositional analysis viciously circular.

8

The Problem of Simple Minds: Is There Anything It Is Like to Be a Honey Bee?

Are frogs conscious? Or fish? What about honey bees? Do paramecia have experiences? Somewhere down the phylogenetic scale phenomenal consciousness ceases. But where? That is the topic of this chapter. It is sometimes supposed that once we begin to reflect upon much simpler beings than ourselves—snails, for example—we are left with nothing physical or structural that we could plausibly take to help us determine whether they are conscious. The Problem of Other Minds, as it applies to the consciousness of such creatures, is without solution. There is really *no* way of our knowing if spiders are conscious of anything as they spin their webs, or if fish undergo any phenomenal experiences as they swim about in the sea.

This pessimistic assessment has led some philosophers to conclude that there is no fact of the matter about whether octupi or toads are conscious, and hence that their consciousness is of no moral importance (Papineau 1994, p. 128). The verificationist thinking upon which this line of argument rests seems to me to have little to recommend it. Why should our inability to decide whether consciousness is present in some cases show that there is real indeterminacy in the world with respect to the matter? We are products of nature as much as everything else. The world need no more conform to our cognitive limitations than it need to those of the simpler creatures at issue. And is it really true anyway that the evident physical and structural differences between ourselves and much more primitive creatures prevent us from knowing whether they are conscious? Is the Problem of Simple Minds, as we might call it, beyond solution?

I say not. Given the theoretical perspective I favor, we are now in a position to determine in general terms where, on the phylogenetic scale, phenomenal consciousness disappears and to make decisions about particular cases. Honey bees, I shall argue, are phenomenally conscious, as are fish; amoeba are not. Amoeba are *zombies*, living things without any "qualia" at all. I begin with a general discussion of the biological function of phenomenal consciousness.

8.1   The Phenomenal Consciousness of Simple Creatures

According to the approach I have argued for at length (Tye 1995 and the chapters in this volume), a mental state is phenomenally conscious just in case it has a PANIC—a Poised, Abstract, Nonconceptual, Intentional Content. Moreover, its phenomenal character or felt aspect is one and the same as its PANIC. My claim thus is that consciousness ceases on the phylogenetic scale with the disappearance of inner states with PANIC. But where does that occur?

States with PANIC are nonconceptual states that track certain features, internal or external, under optimal conditions (and thereby represent those features). They are also states that stand ready and available to make a direct difference to beliefs and desires. It follows that creatures that are incapable of reasoning, of changing their behavior in light of assessments they make, based upon information provided to them by sensory stimulation of one sort or another, are not phenomenally conscious. Tropistic organisms, on this view, feel and experience nothing. They are full-fledged unconscious automata or zombies, rather as blindsight subjects are restricted unconcious automata or partial zombies with respect to a range of visual stimuli.

Consider, to begin with, the case of plants. There are many different sorts of plant behavior; some plants climb, others eat flies, still others eject seeds; many plants close their leaves at night. The immediate cause of these activities is something internal to the plants. Seeds are ejected because of the hydration or dehydration of the cell walls in seed pods. Leaves are closed because of water movement in the stems and petioles of the leaves, itself induced by changes in the temperature and light. These inner events or states are surely not phenomenally conscious. There is nothing it is like to be a venus flytrap or a morning glory.

The behavior of plants is inflexible. It is genetically determined and, therefore, not modifiable by learning. Natural selection has favored the behavior, since historically it has been beneficial to the plant species. But it need not be now. If, for example, flies start to carry on their wings some substance that sickens venus flytraps for several days afterward, this will not have any effect on the plant behavior with respect to flies. Each venus flytrap will continue to snap at flies as long as it has the strength to do so.

Plants do not learn from experience. They neither acquire beliefs and change them in light of things that happen to them nor do they have any desires. To be sure, we sometimes speak as if they do. We say that the wilting daffodils are just begging to be watered. But we recognize full well that this is a harmless *façon de parler*. What we mean is that the daffodils *need* water. There is here no goal-directed behavior, no purpose, nothing that is the result of any learning, no desire *for* water.

Plants, then, are not subject to any PANIC states. Nothing that goes on inside them is poised to make a difference to what they believe or desire. They have no beliefs or desires. So, plants are not phenomenally conscious.

Consider next the case of paramecia. These are simple, unicellular organisms that move toward and engulf food. Changes in light, temperature, electric current, acidity, all elicit immediate, automatic responses, with no flexibility in behavior at all and no salient difference from the case of plants.

What about caterpillars? Is there anything it is like to be a caterpillar? Different kinds of caterpillars show different sorts of behavior upon hatching (Eliot and Soule, 1902). Some, for example, eat the shells of the eggs from which they emerge; others crawl away from their cells immediately. But there is no clear reason to suppose that caterpillars are anything more than stimulus-response devices. They have a very limited range of behaviors available to them, each of which is automatically triggered at the appropriate time by the appropriate stimulus. Consider, for example, their sensitivity to light. Caterpillars have two eyes, one on each side of the head. Given equal light on both eyes, they move straight ahead. But given more light on one of the eyes, that side of the body locomotes more slowly. So, when caterpillars move, they tend to move toward the direction of most intense light, which is why caterpillars climb trees all the way to the top; the light there is strongest. Shift the light to the bottom of the tree, and the caterpillar will go down, not up, as it usually does, even if it means starving to death. Remove one of its eyes, and it will travel in a circle without ever changing its route.[1]

Once one is made aware of these facts, there seems no more reason intuitively to attribute phenomenal consciousness to a caterpillar on the basis of how it moves than to an automatic door. The latter responds in a fixed, mechanical way to the presence of pressure on a plate in the floor or ground in front of it, just as the former responds mechanically to the presence of light. No learning, no variation in behavior with changed circumstances, no reasoned assessment occurs.

Again, this is the result the PANIC theory delivers. Caterpillars do not move purposefully. They do not believe that the light is strongest at the tops of trees. They do not want to get to the strongest light. Nothing in any of their behavior seems to require the admission that they have any wants or beliefs. Caterpillars, then, do not support states with PANIC any more than plants do.

Let us now leave the realm of plants and insects, for the moment, and switch to the case of fish. Fish have eyes, ears, and noses. They also have an acute sense of "distant touch" (Nikolsky 1963), which makes fish in a pond so hard to catch by hand. Place your fingers in water and move them, and you will cause a ripple effect. Fish can detect ripples and currents in water by means of a lateral line that runs down each side of their bodies. The line is a channel under the skin with external openings every so often to the water above. Clumps of protuding sensory hair cells are also attached to it at intervals. As water ripples along the line, it stimulates the hair cells, thereby enabling the fish to detect water currents made by fingers or other fish or by water flowing around obstacles or rocks.[2]

Do fish *feel* anything as water currents are registered by their lateral lines? To the extent that the fish can only respond blindly to the deliverances of their sensory hair cells in a fixed, automatic fashion, there seems to be nothing more than a reflex here, no genuine feeling at all.[3] In these circumstances, the fish has a hard-wired, water-current detector and no more. The fish is like a thermostat, an automatic door opener, a speedometer pointer. There is stimulus and response. But fish do not typically react in a purely reflexive manner. The behavior they produce often depends upon their evaluations or judgments of the deliverances of their senses and their immediate goals (Kirk 1994). These evaluations, in turn, depend to some extent, upon their life histories. This needs a little explanation.

As fish explore, they learn by trial and error. For example, gray snapper include the silverside fish as a standard part of their diets; but when artificially colored silversides were injected with a chemical that made them unpalatable, gray salmon quickly learned to avoid them (while continuing to eat silversides with their natural colors). They also remembered the lesson for substantial periods of time (Reighard 1908).

In another experiment, minnows in one part of an aquarium were separated from a bass by a glass plate (Marshall 1966). The bass initially tried to attack the minnows, but the plate prevented it from reaching them. The result was that the bass eventually stopped trying, even after the glass plate was withdrawn, choosing instead to hunt elsewhere.

Sticklebacks can learn to find indirect routes to food, as the following comments from E. S. Russell (1934) illustrate:

A year or two ago I spent some time training sticklebacks to take food out of a small glass jar placed at the bottom of their aquarium. This sounds like an easy problem, but it proved difficult at first, for the reason that sticklebacks, being visual feeders, were strongly attracted by the sight of food, and spent a long time in the first few trials in fruitless efforts to seize the food through the glass. This prevented them at first from making the simple detour over the rim of the jar which would lead them to the food. With one exception they all solved the problem by chance after one or two tests. Having desisted from the fruitless direct attacks, they swam about through the tank, and happening to pass over the mouth saw the food in the jar from above and darted straight down into the jar and ate it. After a very few chance successes of this kind their behavior changed; they alternated with a direct attack through the glass, definite rises towards the rim of the jar, going in over the edge after a few of these rises; as time went on entry was effected more rapidly, until in the end the fish sometimes went directly to the mouth of the jar and straight in. They had learned to resist the direct attraction of the food and to take the roundabout route.

Fish also come to discriminate fixed features of their territories and to employ them as guides. For example, a light was positioned over a region of a circular tank by its side, and minnows were trained to feed there (Marshall 1966). When the tank was rotated through 180 degrees without moving the light, the fish searched for food at the opposite side to the light. Subsequent tests showed that the minnows were using fine solder marks and oxidation patterns on the side of the tank as indicators.

Pattern recognition in fish is reasonably well developed. Sticklebacks can be trained to distinguish squares from triangles, and will continue to distinguish them through rotations of 30 degrees.[4] Fish can also find their ways through mazes to food, although they do better at this in groups than singly. And in groups, fish who are better at solving mazes tend to take the lead.

Fish, then, exhibit a variety of learned behaviors. They learn to recognize markings and patterns, to avoid artificially colored, unpleasant-tasting fish they would normally eat, to solve problems in order to reach feeding places. Cumulatively, the evidence seems best explained by supposing that fish often make cognitive classifications or assessments directly in response to the information conveyed to them by their senses, and that these, together with their goals, often determine their behavior.

There may be some reluctance to say that fish have beliefs. Clearly, a fish cannot believe that a hand is dangling in the water. Fish lack the concept *hand*. And, in general, it seems unlikely that fish share many concepts with us. But the fact that there are striking conceptual differences, that our concepts are much richer and more articulated than theirs, does not show that they lack any concepts at all. Possessing a perceptual concept, in my view, is (very roughly) a matter of having a stored memory representation that has been acquired through the use of sense organs and is available for retrieval, thereby enabling a range of discriminations to take place.[5] Perceptual beliefs are (roughly) representational states that bring to bear such concepts upon stimuli and that interact in rational ways, however simple, with one another and other representational states the creature generates in response to its needs, thereby determining behavior. Perceptual beliefs are like inner maps by which the creature steers.[6] They function as guides to behavior and do so because of the information (or misinformation) they convey to the creature about what is out there in its environment.[7]

In this sense, given the facts adumbrated earlier about fish behavior, it seems to me very plausible to suppose that fish form simple beliefs on the basis of immediate, sensory representations of their environments. And this certainly is the sense of "belief" I was assuming when I claimed that phenomenal states must be poised to make a direct impact on beliefs and/or desires. So, fish are the subjects of states with PANIC. They are phenomenally conscious.[8]

It is sometimes supposed that for a creature to have beliefs, it must be capable of recognizing its mistakes and changing its behavior in light of that recognition. Without such a capacity, the creature could not be said to be acting rationally or for a reason. But recognition of a mistaken belief requires a second-order belief that the relevant first-order belief is false. So, for a creature to have any beliefs, it must have beliefs about beliefs. And fish surely do not have any beliefs like that.

A view of this sort is held by Donald Davidson. He comments that "in order to have any propositional attitudes at all (specifically beliefs), it is necessary to have the concept of a belief, to have a belief about a belief" (1982, p. 321).

This seems to me an unreasonably strong requirement. Certainly, as I have already emphasized, we do not want to attribute beliefs to explain inflexible behavior. A creature does not act for a reason if its behavior never changes, come what may. And a creature does not act on a false belief if its behavior remains exactly the same, even in the light of evidence that would disconfirm that belief (Bennett 1964). But where beliefs change, and thereby behavior, we need not suppose that a second-order belief is always present.

Suppose, for example, I believe that my car has been stolen upon finding it missing in the carpark. I start to walk to the security office on campus. As I do so, I see my car parked on the other side of the street, and I suddenly remember that I left it there on this occasion. No longer believing that my car has been stolen, I change direction and head directly to it. Here surely I revise my beliefs in light of my perceptual evidence and thereby my behavior. But I need not have any (explicit) belief about a belief. In this sense, I need not (explicitly) recognize my mistake: I need not consider my *belief* that my car has been stolen as such at all. I am certainly acting for reasons, however; and as my reasons change, my behavior changes too.

Of course, if you asked me whether I believed that my earlier belief was false, I would respond affirmatively. But what I then believe when I am asked the question is not necessarily what I did believe before. If you asked me now whether 9 cubed minus 17 is the same as 712, I would pause and then say "Yes." But I didn't (explicitly) believe that at any earlier time.

Now fish can, and do, change their behavior as their evidence changes. Moreover, these changes are often best explained by reference to simple beliefs or assessments, and they are relevant to hypotheses we may form about what the fish believe before and after. The fact that they are incapable of reflecting upon their erroneous beliefs matters not at all to the more fundamental question of whether they are believers.

I come finally to the case of honey bees. There are many examples of sophisticated honey bee behavior. Bee colonies take on odors, primarily as a result of the food contained in the hives. These odors, which vary from hive to hive, are absorbed by the fur on the bees, and guards, placed at the entrance to the hive, learn to use it to check whether incoming bees are intruders or members of the colony. Scouts fly out from the hive each spring in search of a cavity suitable for a new hive. They use the sun as their main guide but they also rely upon landmarks. Upon returning, they dance to show bees in the hive what they have discovered. Their dance requires them to remember how the sun moves relative to the positions of the landmarks, enabling them to communicate the position of the cavity correctly. Recruit bees must learn what the dancers are telling them. This demands that they form some sort of cognitive map involving the landmarks. Scouts back from their trips attend to the dances of other scouts and then go out again to visit the different cavities. With their later return, they dance again. Eventually, the dances agree and the colony moves as one to the chosen spot (Gould 1979).

Of course, some of this is preprogrammed. Bees choose neither to dance nor how to navigate; these activities are instinctive. But, equally clearly, in the above examples, the bees learn and use facts about their environments as they go along. How the bees dance is guided by information they have acquired about the location of the new cavity, the positions of landmarks, and so forth; moreover, this information is grasped by the bees who attend the dances and it, in turn, guides their behavior.

Honey bees are very good at detecting and remembering odors. Karl Von Frisch showed that they can identify one odor among 700 others,[9] and their memory has been tested to last over half a year. Honey bees also have short-term memory stores, which can be disrupted just as those of humans can be. When they find a new food source, and they are shocked within five minutes of their discovery, they completely forget it. If the shock is delivered after 10 minutes, they go back to the food source. The former behavior is like that of people who lose their memory of a violent accident immediately afterward.

Children who are starting to learn the alphabet can discriminate different letters, whatever their size or font. Pigeons can be trained to do this also. So, too, can honey bees up to a point. Some bees can recognize the letter B in different orientations, colors, sizes, and fonts (Gould and Gould 1988).[10] Apparently, then, they can form novel concepts of items not normally found in their natural habitats.

Here is a striking example of apparently intelligent behavior in honey bees.[11] The flowers of alfalfa possess anthers that spring forward and deliver a heavy blow in response to pressure. Once honey bees have been hit by the alfalfa anther, they avoid alfalfa like the plague. But if they are taken to a region of many acres of alfalfa and set free there, they are compelled to confront the problem or starve to death. So, they do one of two things: either they learn to identify flowers, the anthers of which have already sprung, and they only alight on the sprung ones; or they learn to get at the nectar by chewing through the flower from the side without ever setting off the anther.

Perhaps this behavior is not as intelligent as it first appears (Gould and Gould 1988, p. 221). Bees often feed from the sides of flowers when the structure of the flower is such that the bees' tongues cannot reach the nectar, and perhaps this behavior is preprogrammed. Even so, the bees do learn to identify the tripped alfalfa and they only resort to the side-feeding tactic after they have been hit by an anther. Therefore, the applicability of the technique to this case is something that they learn.

A final example is provided by an experiment in which bees were shown some sugar solution on a plate near the hive. Then every five minutes or so, the plate was moved away so that the distance from the hive increased by one quarter. Initially, with the plate only four inches away, it was moved just one inch. But later when the food was four hundred feet away, the plate was removed another 100 feet. Amazingly, the bees caught on to this procedure and began to anticipate where the sugar would be next by flying there and waiting for the plate to arrive!

There seems to be ample evidence, then, that honey bees make decisions about how to behave in response to how things look, taste, and smell. They use the information their senses give them to identify things, to find their way around, to survive. They learn what to do in many cases as the situation demands. Their behavior is sometimes flexible and goal-driven. They are, therefore, the subjects of states with PANIC. Some of the states honey bees undergo are generated by sensory stimulation and make an immediate impact upon their cognitive systems. This being the case, honey bees, like fish, *are* phenomenally conscious: there is *something it is like* for them.

My conclusion is that phenomenal consciousness is not restricted to vertebrates. In my view, it is found wherever there is PANIC. And the evidence strongly suggests that some insects are phenomenally conscious. Where exactly in the insect realm phenomenal consciousness ends I shall not try to say. That would require a detailed case-by-case study of the sort I cannot undertake here. And it may well be that the boundary is fuzzy, that there are some genuinely borderline cases of phenomenal consciousness; but the question certainly seems to me a tractable one, given the theoretical perspective I am defending.

Some philosophers will no doubt respond that the boundary between the creatures that are phenomenally conscious and those that are zombies *cannot* be fuzzy. Conscious experience or feeling is either present or it isn't. The intensity level or richness of a subject's experience can vary—think, for example, of the experiences one undergoes when one is falling asleep or just waking up, and contrast those with the experiences one has when looking at a garden full of flowers on a bright summer's day. In each case, however, there is *something it is like* for the subject. No matter how low the intensity of the experience, if there is any experience at all, phenomenal consciousness is still present.

This conception of phenomenal consciousness gives rise to the comparison with an inner light (e.g., McGinn 1982). Light beams can vary in their intensity; moreover, as the intensity of a given beam is reduced, although it may become hard to say just when the light is fully extinguished, there is a definite fact of the matter about when the light completely disappears. At some precise point, no light is left at all.

I reject the inner light picture. It seems to me that we can make sense of the idea of a borderline experience. Suppose you are participating in a psychological experiment and you are listening to quieter and quieter sounds through headphones. As the process continues, a point may come at which you are unsure whether you hear anything at all. Now it could be that there is a still a fact of the matter here (as on the dimming light model); but, equally, it could be that whether you still hear anything is objectively indeterminate. So, it could be that there is no fact of the matter about whether there is anything it is like for you to be in the state you are in at that time. In short, it could be that you are undergoing a borderline experience.

In the final section, I want to issue some disclaimers with respect to what I have committed myself to so far.

8.2   Some Disclaimers

To begin with, nothing in the picture of phenomenal consciousness I have sketched demands that phenomenally conscious states be *introspectible*. I am certainly not committed to the view that honey bees can introspect any of the contents of their minds. Simpler creatures, like fish or honey bees, have sense organs that respond to the outside world, bodies that allow them to move in their environments, and inner experiences that causally trigger simple beliefs and decisions. But they need not also have the capacity to be conscious of their mental states, to tell what is going on in their minds. That, we may suppose, evolved only in more complex organisms.[12]

On this view, honey bees and fish behave intelligently and they are the subject of phenomenally conscious experiences, but they have no

higher-order consciousness. In the higher-order sense, they are unconscious automata—they have no *cognitive* awareness of their sensory
states. They do not bring their own *experiences* under concepts. Unlike
you and I, they function perpetually in a state like that of the woman
who is lost in thought about how to overcome her financial difficulties
as she sits in her garden. During the period of contemplation, the woman
has her eyes open. She sees the lawn and the flower beds before her. But
she is not aware of her visual sensations. She is not paying any attention
to them. In short, she has no thoughts about her perceptions, about how
things phenomenally *look* to her: her thoughts lie elsewhere.

Consciousness of the sort this woman lacks is not phenomenal consciousness. Her blindness is cognitive: she is oblivious to the phenomenal character of her visual states. But those states still have such a
character. Things do not lose their looks to her while she ponders how
to solve her financial problems. The roses in her field of view still look
red even if she does not *notice* how they look.

If indeed simple creatures like honey bees are inherently blind to their
inner states, then, although they are the subjects of phenomenal consciousness, they never *suffer*. Suffering requires the cognitive awareness
of pain. The person who has a bad headache and who is distracted for
a moment or two does not suffer at that time. The headache continues
to exist—briefly not noticing it does not eliminate it—but there is no cognitive awareness of pain and hence no suffering. In the phenomenal
sense, however, the pain still exists even though its subject is briefly blind
to it.

I conclude that the thesis that simple creatures are phenomenally conscious does not commit me to any strong thesis about how we should
behave toward them. Whether or not simple creatures feel pain, without
the power to introspect they do not suffer.

This brings me to my third and final point. Consider the following
case. I do not realize that the top of the stove is hot. Upon touching it,
I quickly withdraw my hand, feeling sudden pain as I do so. The pain
here does not really make a difference to my withdrawal behavior. With-
drawing the hand is a reflex that is routed directly through the spinal
cord without the intervention of the brain. Of course, the message from
the damaged tissue also goes to the brain and produces the sensation of
pain. But the pain does not cause the reflexive withdrawal of my hand.

In these circumstances, my phenomenal state is causally irrelevant with respect to my immediate, actual behavior. How, then, can it be a state with PANIC? More generally, does not the account I have offered entail that *wherever* a creature behaves reflexively, there cannot be any associated phenomenal state?

Again, this is no consequence of my view. Nothing in my account requires that experiences and feelings always make an actual difference with respect to behavior. A state can be poised to make a difference without, in fact, doing so. In the case of the pain I feel from touching the stove, I am hardwired to react behaviorally before my awareness of pain elicits any response. But the pain is registered by my cognitive centers. So, there is an actual difference in my beliefs and desires: for example, I believe that I am in pain; I want the pain to go away. This change in my beliefs and desires is likely reflected in my *subsequent* behavior—for example, my putting my hand under cold water, my going to the medicine cabinet, and so on. Moreover, had the reflex that causes me to pull my hand away failed, the way the pain felt would have caused me to do just what I actually did, only a fraction of a second later.[13]

The phenomenal character of my pain, then, not only is poised to make a cognitive difference but also actually makes such a difference, even though my immediate behavior is reflexive. And it is, of course, from experiences of this sort that I learn to avoid things that damage my body. These simple facts pose no threat to the PANIC theory.

The upshot, I suggest, is that there is nothing especially mysterious or counterintuitive in the idea that much simpler creatures than ourselves undergo phenomenal states. This does not commit us to supposing that these creatures are reflective in the ways that we are. Nor does it even commit us to supposing that they have any awareness of their experiences at all. Moreover, the presence of phenomenal states does not automatically rule out the presence of *some* reflexive behavior.

Notes

1. This example is from Rachlin (1976), cited in Dretske (1988).

2. Some fish have electrosensors. These are modifications of the sensors in the lateral line (and are most frequently found on the head).

3. For more on reflexes and experience, see section 8.2.

4. At 45 degrees, they do much worse, and at greater angles, they are unable to perform the discriminations at all (Marshall 1966, p. 241). This shows that their responses were cued to some combination of figure and orientation and not just to shape alone.

5. Of course, concepts are fine-grained. The concept F can be different from the concept G, even when they have the same extensions. The relevant discriminations for the concept F are those that are made with respect to objects' *being F*. Where every object that is F is also G and vice versa, it may be very difficult, in some cases, to decide which of the two concepts is being exercised. After all, if the creature lacks a language, then we cannot resort to questions about what would have been said with respect to the presented object in the counterfactual situation in which the object has one of the properties without the other. Still, it seems to me, there can be a fact of the matter here. For example, it will not be true that the concept F is the one the creature actually exercises in response to things that are both F and G, if the creature *would have* behaved selectively just as it actually does, *had* it been presented with things that were G and not F in otherwise similar circumstances.

6. This comparison is from Frank Ramsey (1931). I should add that, in my view, perceptual beliefs do not *literally* have a topographic or maplike internal structure.

7. For more on this model of belief, see Dretske (1988).

8. In my earlier remarks on learning, I did not mean to suggest that wherever there is any learning, however broadly construed, there are automatically beliefs. If learning is taken *very* loosely to be any behavioral change, then behavioral transformations brought about by such things as a knee injury or receptor fatigue count as learning. In these cases, there is no appropriate inner representation, no internal "map," the content of which explains the behavior produced by such changes.

9. However, there are also striking limitations. Honeybees cannot learn the odor of a flower except when they are on it (Menzel and Erber 1978).

10. However, when complex distracting backgrounds involving abstract shapes are introduced, only one bee (as of 1988) successfully identified the letter B in a novel font (Gould and Gould 1988, p. 219).

11. This example, and the one that follows, are both taken from Gould (1979).

12. What introspection of experiences gives to organisms that are capable of it is increased malleability or flexibility in behavior. If I can introspect how things appear to me, I can form beliefs about how things appear. This, then, permits me to decide whether my perceptual experiences are accurate, whether the world really is as it appears to be. So, I need not be guided blindly in my beliefs about the way the world is by the appearances alone. I am not compelled to take my perceptual experiences at face value. I can come to the conclusion that things are *not* as they appear, and I can change my behavior accordingly. The range of alternative actions available to me thereby expands. I am also at an advantage with

respect to organisms that lack introspection. Given the cognitive means to withhold assent to experiences I judge to be misleading, I can choose not to act in circumstances in which an organism without the power to introspect would unhesitatingly move ahead. My chances of survival, therefore, are greater (other things being equal).

13. Assuming, of course, that, at that time, the relevant nerves controlling the pain behavior were operating properly again.

References

Armstrong, D. 1962. *Bodily Sensations*. London: Routledge and Kegan Paul.

Armstrong, D. 1968. *A Materialist Theory of Mind*. London: Routledge and Kegan Paul.

Armstrong, D. 1997. Smart and the Secondary Qualities. In A. Byrne and D. Hilbert (1997). *Readings on Color*, Vol. 1, Cambridge, Mass.

Baron-Cohen, S. 1995. *Mindblindness*. Cambridge, Mass.: MIT Press, Bradford Books.

Bennett, J. 1964. *Rationality*. London: Routledge and Kegan Paul.

Block, N. 1983. The Photographic Fallacy in the Debate about Mental Imagery. *Nous*, 654–64.

Block, N. 1990. Inverted Earth. *Philosophical Perspectives* 4, ed. J. Tomberlin. Northridge, Calif.: Ridgeview.

Block, N. 1993. Review of D. Dennett, *Consciousness Explained*, *Journal of Philosophy* 90: 181–93.

Block, N. 1995. On A Confusion about a Function of Consciousness. *Behavioral and Brain Sciences* 18: 227–47.

Block, N. 1996. Mental Paint and Mental Latex. *Philosophical Issues* 7, ed. E. Villenueva. Northridge, Calif.: Ridgeview.

Block, N. 1998. Is Experience Just Representing? *Philosophy and Phenomenological Research* 58: 663–70.

Block, N. 1999a. Sexism, Racism, Ageism, and the Nature of Consciousness. In *The Philosophy of Sydney Shoemaker, Philosophical Topics*, 26 (1 and 2).

Block, N., and Stalnaker, S. 1999b. Conceptual Analysis, Dualism, and the Explanatory Gap. *Philosophical Review* 180: 1–46.

Boghossian, P. 1994. The Transparency of Mental Content. *Philosophical Perspectives* 8, ed. J. Tomberlin. Northridge, Calif.: Ridgeview.

Boghossian, P., and Velleman, D. 1989. Color as a Secondary Quality. *Mind* 98: 81–103.

Brentano, F. 1973. Psychology From an Empirical Standpoint. New York: Humanities (originally published 1874).

Broad, C. 1923. *Scientific Thought*. London: Routledge and Kegan Paul.

Byrne, A., and Hilbert, D. 1997. *Readings on Color*, Vol. 1. Cambridge, Mass.: MIT Press, Bradford Books.

Campbell, J. 1997. A Simple View of Color. In *Readings on Color*, Vol. 1, ed. A. Byrne and D. Hilbert. Cambridge, Mass.: MIT Press, Bradford Books.

Chalmers, D. 1996. *The Conscious Mind*. Oxford: Oxford University Press.

Chisholm, R. 1957. *Perceiving: A Philosophical Study*. Ithaca, N.Y.: Cornell University Press.

Cosmides, L., and Tooby, J. 1995. Foreword to S. Baron-Cohen, *Mindblindness*. Cambridge, Mass.: MIT Press, Bradford Books.

Davidson, D. 1982. Rational Animals. *Dialectica* 36: 318–27.

DeBellis, M. 1991. The Representational Content of Musical Experience. *Philosophy and Phenomenological Research* 51: 303–24.

Dretske, F. 1988. *Explaining Behavior*. Cambridge, Mass.: MIT Press, Bradford Books.

Dretske, F. 1995. *Naturalizing the Mind*. Cambridge, Mass.: MIT Press, Bradford Books.

DuBois-Reymond, E. 1885–1887. *Reden*, Leipzig.

Efron, R. 1968. What is Perception? *Boston Studies in Philosophy of Science* 4: 159.

Eliot, I., and Soule, C. 1902. *Caterpillars and Their Moths*. New York: Century.

Fodor, J. 1990. A Theory of Content I and II. In *A Theory of Content and Other Essays*. Cambridge, Mass.: MIT Press, Bradford Books.

Gibbard, A. 1996. Visible Properties of Human Interest Only. *Philosophical Issues*, ed. E. Villenueva. Atascadero, Calif.: Ridgeview.

Gould, J. 1979. Do Honeybees Know What They Are Doing? *Natural History* 6: 66–75.

Gould, J., and Gould, C. 1988. *The Honey Bee*. New York: Scientific American Library.

Grandy, R. 1989. A Modern Inquiry into the Physical Reality of Colors. In *Mind, Value, and Culture: Essays in Honor of E.M. Adams*, ed. D. Weissbord. Atascadero, Calif.: Ridgeview.

Gregory, R. 1990. *Eye and Brain*. London: Weidenfeld and Nicolson.

Hardin, L. 1988. *Color for Philosophers*. Indianapolis: Hackett.

Hardin, L. 1997. Reinverting the Spectrum. In *Readings on Color*, Vol. 1, ed. A. Byrne and D. Hilbert. Cambridge, Mass.: MIT Press, Bradford Books.

Harman, G. 1990. The Intrinsic Quality of Experience. In *Philosophical Perspectives* 4, ed. J. Tomberlin. Northridge, Calif.: Ridgeview.

Harman, G. 1996. Qualia and Color Concepts. *Philosophical Issues* 7, ed. E. Villenueva. Northridge, Calif.: Ridgeview.

Hilbert, D. 1987. *Color and Color Perception: A Study in Anthropocentric Realism.* Stanford: Center for the Study of Language and Information.

Horgan, T. 1984. Jackson on Physical Information and Qualia. *Philosophical Quarterly* 34: 147–83.

Hurvich, L. 1981. *Color Vision.* Sunderland, Mass.: Sinaeur Associates.

Jackendoff, R. 1989. *Consciousness and the Computational Mind.* Cambridge, Mass.: MIT Press, Bradford Books.

Jackson, F. 1977. *Perception.* Cambridge: Cambridge University Press.

Jackson, F. 1982. Epiphenomenal Qualia. *Philosophical Quarterly* 32: 127–36.

Jackson, F. 1993. Armchair Metaphysics. In *Philosophy of Mind*, ed. J. O'Leary-Hawthorne and M. Michael. Dordrecht, Holland: Kluwer Books.

Jackson, F., and Pargetter, R. 1997. An Objectivist's Guide to Subjectivism about Color. In *Readings on Color*, Vol. 1, ed. A. Byrne and D. Hilbert. Cambridge Mass.: MIT Press, Bradford Books.

Johnston, M. 1992. How to Speak of the Colors. *Philosophical Studies*, 68: 221–63.

Kirk, R. 1994. *Raw Feeling.* Oxford: Clarendon Press.

Kosslyn, S. 1980. *Image and Mind.* Cambridge, Mass: Harvard University Press.

Kosslyn, S. 1994. *Image and Brain.* Cambridge, Mass: Harvard University Press.

Kripke, S. 1972. Naming and Necessity. In *Semantics of Natural Language*, ed. D. Davidson and G. Harman. Dordrecht, Holland: Reidel, 253–355.

Kuehni, R. 1997. *Color.* New York: J. Wiley and Sons.

Landis, T., Graves, R., Benson, F., and Hebben, N. 1982. Visual Recognition through Kinaesthetic Mediation. *Psychological Medicine* 12: 515–31.

Levin, J. 1990. Could Love Be Like a Heat-Wave? Physicalism and the Subjective Character of Experience. In *Mind and Cognition: A Reader*, ed. W. Lycan. Oxford: Blackwell.

Levine, J. 1983, Materialism and Qualia: The Explanatory Gap. *Pacific Philosophical Quarterly* 64: 354–61.

Lewis, D. 1983a. Mad Pain and Martian Pain. In his *Philosophical Papers*, Vol. 1. Oxford: Oxford University Press.

Lewis, D. 1983b. Postscript to "Mad Pain and Martian Pain," in his *Philosophical Papers*, Vol. 1. Oxford: Oxford University Press.

Lewis, D. 1990. What Experience Teaches. In *Mind and Cognition: A Reader*, ed. W. Lycan. Oxford: Blackwell.

Loar, B. 1990. Phenomenal States. In *Philosophical Perspectives* 4, ed. J. Tomberlin. Northridge, Calif.: Ridgeview.

Lycan, W. 1996a. Layered Perceptual Representation. *Philosophical Issues* 7, ed. E. Villeneuva. Northridge, Calif.: Ridgeview.

Lycan, W. 1996b. *Consciousness and Experience*. Cambridge, Mass.: MIT Press, Bradford Books.

Mackie, J. 1976. Primary and Secondary Qualities. In *Problems from Locke*. Oxford: Oxford University Press.

Marshall, N. 1966. *The Life of Fishes*. New York: The World Publishing Company.

McDowell, J. 1994. The Content of Perceptual Experience. *Philosophical Quarterly*, 44.

McGinn, C. 1982. *The Character of Mind*. Oxford: Oxford University Press.

McGinn, C. 1991. *The Problem of Consciousness*. Oxford: Blackwell.

Marr, D. 1982. *Vision*. San Francisco: W. H. Freeman.

McGinn, C. 1991. *The Problem of Consciousness*. Oxford: Blackwell.

McGinn, C. 1997. Another Look at Color. *Journal of Philosophy* 93: 537–53.

McLaughlin, B., and Tye, M. 1998. Externalism, Twin-earth, and Self-Knowledge. In *Knowing Our Own Minds: Essays on Self-Knowledge*, ed. C. Macdonald, B. Smith, and C. Wright. Oxford: Oxford University Press.

Meinong, A. 1960. The Theory of Objects. In *Realism and the Background of Phenomenology*, ed. R. Chisholm. Glencoe, Ill.: Free Press.

Menzel, R., and Erber, J. 1978. Learning and Memory in Honey Bees. *Scientific American* 239: 101–11.

Moore, G. 1903. The Refutation of Idealism. In *Philosophical Papers*. London: Routledge and Kegan Paul.

Nagel, T. 1974. What Is It Like to Be a Bat? *Philosophical Review* 83: 435–56.

Nemirow, L. 1980. Review of Nagel's *Mortal Questions*. *Philosophical Review* 89: 473–77.

Nemirow, L. 1990. Physicalism and the Cognitive Role of Acquaintance. In *Mind and Cognition: A Reader*, ed. W. Lycan. Oxford: Blackwell.

Nikolsky, G. 1963. *The Ecology of Fishes*. New York: Academic Press.

Papineau, D. 1994. *Naturalism*. Oxford: Blackwell.

Peacocke, C. 1983. *Sense and Content*. Oxford: Oxford University Press.

Peacocke, C. 1992. Scenarios, Concepts, and Perception. In *The Contents of Experience: Essays on Perception*, ed. T. Crane. Cambridge: Cambridge University Press, 105–35.

Peacocke, C. 1993. Review of M. Tye, *The Imagery Debate*. *Philosophy of Science*, 675–7.

Perky, C. 1910. An Experimental Study of the Imagination. *American Journal of Psychology* 21: 422–52.

Rachlin, H. 1976. *Behavior and Learning*. San Francisco: Freeman.

Raffmann, D. 1996. On the Persistence of Phenomenology. In *Conscious Experience*, ed. T. Metzinger. Paderborn, Germany: Schoning-Verlag Press.

Ramsey, F. 1931. *The Foundations of Mathematics and Other Logical Essays*. London: Routledge and Kegan Paul.

Reighard, J. 1908. An Experimental Field-study of Warning Colouration in Coral Reef Fishes. *Carnegie Institute of Washington* 2: 257–325.

Reisberg, D. 1987. Visual Imagery and Memory for Appearance: Does Clark Gable or George C. Scott Have Bushier Eyebrows? *Canadian Journal of Psychology* 41: 521–6.

Rey, G. 1992. Sensational Sentences. In *Consciousness: Psychological and Philosophical Essays*, ed. M. Davies and G. Humphreys. Oxford: Blackwell.

Rey, G. 1991. Sensations in a Language of Thought. *Philosophical Issues* 2, ed. E. Villeneuva, Northridge, Calif.: Ridgeview.

Rock, I. 1983. *The Logic of Perception*. Cambridge, Mass.: MIT Press, Bradford Books.

Rosenthal, D. 1986. Two Concepts of Consciousness. *Philosophical Studies*, 49, 329–59.

Russell, B. 1912. *The Problems of Philosophy*, New York: Henry Holf.

Russell, E. 1934. *The Behavior of Animals*. London: Edward Arnolf.

Sacks, O. 1996. *The Island of the Colorblind*. New York: Alfred A. Knopf.

Searle, J. 1992. *The Rediscovery of Mind*. Cambridge, Mass: MIT Press, Bradford Books.

Shepard, R. 1997. The Perceptual Organization of Colors: An Adaptation to Regularities of the Terrestrial World. In *Readings on Color*, Vol. 2, ed. A. Byrne and D. Hilbert. Cambridge, Mass.: MIT Press, Bradford Books.

Shoemaker, S. 1990. Qualities and Qualia: What's in the Mind. *Philosophy and Phenomenological Research* 50, Supplement, 109–31.

Shoemaker, S. 1994. Phenomenal Character. *Nous* 28: 21–38.

Shoemaker, S. 1996. Lecture III: The Phenomenal Character of Experience. In his *The First-Person Respective and Other Essays*, New York: Cambridge Univ. Press.

Shoemaker, S. 2000. Phenomenal Character Revisited, *Philosophy and Phenomenological Research* 60.

Smart, J. 1997. On Some Criticisms of a Physicalist Theory of Colors. In *Readings on Color*, Vol. 1, ed. A. Byrne and D. Hilbert. Cambridge, Mass.: MIT Press, Bradford Books.

Stalnaker, R. 1984. *Inquiry*. Cambridge, Mass.: MIT Press, Bradford Books.

Stampe, D. 1977. Towards a Causal Theory of Linguistic Representation. *Midwest Studies in Philosophy* 2: 42–63.

___ Sturgeon, S. 1994. The Epistemic View of Subjectivity. *Journal of Philosophy* 91: 221–35.

___ Tye, M. 1982. A Causal Analysis of Seeing. *Philosophy and Phenomenological Research* 42: 311–25.

___ Tye, M. 1986. The Subjective Qualities of Experience. *Mind* 95: 1–17.

Tye, M. 1991. *The Imagery Debate*. Cambridge, Mass.: MIT Press, Bradford Books.

Tye, M. 1993. Image Indeterminacy: the Picture Theory of Images and the Bifurcation of 'What' and 'Where' Information in Higher-level Vision. In *Spatial Representation*, ed. N. Eilan, R. McCarthy, and B. Brewer. Oxford: Blackwell.

Tye, M. 1995. *Ten Problems of Consciousness*. Cambridge, Mass.: MIT Press, Bradford Books.

___ Tye, M. 1995b. A Representational Theory of Pains and their Phenomenal Character. *Philosophical Perspectives* 9; also reprinted with revisions in *The Nature of Consciousness: Philosophical and Scientific Debates*, ed. N. Block, O. Flanagan, and G. Guzeldere. Cambridge, Mass.: MIT Press, Bradford Books.

Tye, M. 1996a. The Burning House. In *Conscious Experience*, ed. T. Metzinger. Schoning-Verlag Press.

Tye, M. 1996b. The Function of Consciousness. *Nous* 30.

___ Tye, M. 1996c. Perceptual Experience Is a Many-Layered Thing. *Philosophical Issues* 7, ed. E. Villeneuva. Northridge, Calif.: Ridgeview.

Tye, M. 1998a. Response to Discussants. *Philosophy and Phenomenological Research* 58: 679–87.

___ Tye, M. 1998b. Externalism and Memory. *Proceedings of the Aristotelian Society,* supplementary volume.

Tye, M. 2000. Shoemaker's *The First-Person Perspective and Other Essays*. *Philosophy and Phenomenological Research* 60.

Weiskrantz, L. 1986. *Blindsight: A Case Study and Its Implications*. New York: Oxford University Press.

___ White, S. 1995. Color and the Narrow Contents of Experience. *Philosophical Topics* 23.

Name Index

Subject Index